KEY IRISH WOMEN WRITERS

Series Editors: Kathryn Laing and Sinéad Mooney

1. Clíona Ó Gallchoir, *Maria Edgeworth*
2. Heather Ingman, *Elizabeth Bowen*
3. Aintzane Legarreta Mentxaka, *Kate O'Brien*
4. Eibhear Walshe, *Jane Wilde*

Elizabeth Bowen

Elizabeth Bowen

Heather Ingman

EER
Edward Everett Root, Publishers, Brighton, 2021.

EER
Edward Everett Root, Publishers, Co. Ltd.,
Atlas Chambers, 33 West Street, Brighton, East Sussex, BN1 2RE.
Details of our overseas agents and how to buy our books are given on our website.
www.eerpublishing.com

edwardeverettroot@yahoo.co.uk

Key Irish Women Writers series, volume 2.

© Heather Ingman 2021.

First published in England 2021.

This edition © Edward Everett Root Publishers, 2021.

ISBN: 978-1-913087-37-1 paperback
ISBN: 978-1-913087-38-8 hardback
ISBN: 978-1-913087-39-5 e-book

Heather Ingman has asserted her right to be identified as the owner of the copyright of this Work in accordance with the Copyright, Designs and Patents Act 1988 as the owner of this Work.

All rights reserved. No part of this publication may be reproduced, stored in a retrieval system or transmitted in any form or by any means, electronic, mechanical, photocopying, recording or otherwise, without the prior permission of the copyright owner.

Cover and book production by Pageset Limited, High Wycombe, Buckinghamshire.

Contents

Acknowledgements ix
Abbreviations xi
Biographical Timeline xiii
Introduction: Reading Elizabeth Bowen 1

Chapter One:
    The Female *Bildungsroman*: *The Hotel* and *The Last
    September* 13

Chapter Two:
    Interwar Femininity: *Friends and Relations* and
    To the North. 35

Chapter Three:
    Widening the Scene: *The House in Paris* and
    The Death of the Heart 57

Chapter Four:
    Short Stories 79

Chapter Five:
    Wartime Writing: *Bowen's Court* and *The Heat of
    the Day* 99

Chapter Six:
    Time and Trauma: *A World of Love*, *The Little Girls*,
    and *Eva Trout, or Changing Scenes* 121

Epilogue 151
Bibliography 155
Index 163

The author

HEATHER INGMAN is Visiting Research Fellow in the Centre for Gender and Women's Studies, Trinity College, the University of Dublin and was, until her retirement, Adjunct Professor in the School of English, TCD, where she taught courses on Irish writing and modernist women's fiction. Her most recent publications include *Strangers to Themselves: Ageing in Irish Writing* (Palgrave, 2018), *Irish Women's Fiction from Edgeworth to Enright* (Irish Academic Press, 2013), *A History of the Irish Short Story* (Cambridge University Press, 2009), and *Twentieth-Century Fiction by Irish Women: Nation and Gender* (Ashgate, 2007). She is co-editor, with Clíona Ó Gallchoir, of *A History of Modern Irish Women's Literature* (Cambridge University Press, 2018).

Acknowledgements

I wish to thank the general editors of the *Key Irish Women Writers* series, Sinéad Mooney and Kathryn Laing, for commissioning this book on Elizabeth Bowen and for their support during the writing process. I am grateful to the anonymous reader for insightful observations on the manuscript. I would also like to thank my former colleagues in the School of English, Trinity College, Dublin and successive classes of students who have shared my enthusiasm for Bowen's work. Thanks also to Patricia Coughlan for several stimulating conversations about Bowen over the years on the margins of conferences. Finally, I thank my husband, Ferdinand von Prondzynski, for being a patient sounding board for my ideas about Bowen during the writing process. This book was written before Covid-19 changed all our lives. The final editing was done during lockdown, a time when Bowen, a writer who knew more than most about living through periods of violent change, seemed particularly relevant.

Abbreviations

AFT   *Afterthought: Pieces About Writing* (London: Longmans Green and Co., 1962).
B   *The Bazaar and Other Stories* edited by Allan Hepburn (Edinburgh: Edinburgh University Press, 2008).
BC   *Bowen's Court and Seven Winters* (London: Virago, 1984).
CI   *Collected Impressions* (London: Longmans, Green and Co., 1950).
CS   *Collected Stories* (London: Vintage, 1999).
DH   *The Death of the Heart* (Harmondsworth: Penguin, 1989).
ET   *Eva Trout, or Changing Scenes* (London: Vintage, 1999).
FR   *Friends and Relations* (Harmondsworth: Penguin, 1987).
H   *The Hotel* (Harmondsworth: Penguin, 1987).
HD   *The Heat of the Day* (London: Vintage, 1998).
HP   *The House in Paris* (Harmondsworth: Penguin, 1987).
LCW   *Love's Civil War* edited by Victoria Glendinning, with Judith Robertson (London: Simon and Schuster, 2008).
LG   *The Little Girls* (Harmondsworth: Penguin, 1982).
LI   *Listening In: Broadcasts, Speeches, and Interviews by Elizabeth Bowen* edited by Allan Hepburn (Edinburgh: Edinburgh University Press, 2010).
LS   *The Last September* (Harmondsworth: Penguin, 1987).
MT   *The Mulberry Tree: Writings of Elizabeth Bowen* edited by Hermione Lee (London: Vintage, 1999).

PPT *People, Places, Things: Essays by Elizabeth Bowen* edited by Allan Hepburn (Edinburgh: Edinburgh University Press, 2008).
S *The Shelbourne* (London: Vintage, 2017).
SIW *Elizabeth Bowen's Selected Irish Writings* edited by Eibhear Walshe (Cork: Cork University Press, 2011).
TN *To the North* (London: Vintage, 1999).
TR *A Time in Rome* (London, Vintage, 2010).
WL *A World of Love* (London: Vintage, 1999).

Biographical Timeline

1899 Elizabeth Dorothea Cole Bowen born 7 June in Herbert Place, Dublin, only child of Anglo-Irish parents, Henry Charles Cole Bowen, a barrister, and Florence Colley Bowen from Mount Temple, Dublin. Bowen's childhood alternates between winters in Dublin and summers at the family seat, Bowen's Court, in Co. Cork.

1905 The hereditary Bowen tendency to nervous instability manifests itself when Henry Bowen suffers a serious mental breakdown. The immediate cause is attributed to overwork. Simultaneous to the traumatic events surrounding her father's illness, Elizabeth develops a severe, lifelong stammer.

1906 On Henry's doctors' advice, Florence and Elizabeth move to the Kent coast, staying with Anglo-Irish relations and in seaside villas in Folkestone and Hythe.

1912 Florence dies of cancer. Elizabeth, left in the care of her Colley aunts, is sent to Harpenden Hall school in Hertfordshire, living in term times with her aunt Laura and spending her summers at Bowen's Court with Henry, by now recovered from his breakdown.

1914 Elizabeth is at Bowen's Court with her father and cousin Audrey when World War One breaks out. In September she attends Downe House boarding school in Kent.

1917 Leaves Downe House.

1918 Works in an Irish hospital for shell-shocked veterans. Her father marries Mary Gwynn.

1919 Bowen spends two terms at the London County Council School of Art. Starts writing short stories.
1919–1921 Irish War of Independence.
1921 Engaged to Lieutenant John Anderson, a British officer stationed in Cork. Spends winter in a hotel in Italy with her aunt, Edie Colley, and while there, breaks off her engagement.
1923 With the help of Rose Macaulay, Bowen publishes her first collection of short stories, *Encounters*. In August, marries Alan Cameron, then Assistant Secretary for Education for Northamptonshire. Alan was six years older, had been badly gassed during the First World War, and the marriage is thought not to have been fully consummated.
1925 Bowen and Cameron relocate to Oxford, Alan having been appointed Secretary of Education for the city. Bowen begins to move in literary circles in Oxford and London, getting to know, among others, John Buchan, David Cecil, Maurice Bowra, Isaiah Berlin, Cyril Connolly, Rosamond Lehmann and Virginia Woolf.
1926 *Ann Lee's and Other Stories*.
1927 *The Hotel*.
1929 *The Last September. Joining Charles and Other Stories*.
1930 After a brief return of mental illness, Henry Bowen dies and Bowen inherits Bowen's Court where, from now on, she will spend her summers, often hosting literary house-parties. Becomes a prolific reviewer for periodicals such as *The Times Literary Supplement, New Statesman, Spectator, Tatler*.
1931 *Friends and Relations*.
1932 *To the North*.
1933 Affair with Oxford academic Humphry House who is quoted as saying he took her virginity. The affair survives his marriage to Madeline Church but ends when the Houses move to Calcutta in 1936.

1934 *The Cat Jumps and Other Stories*. Virginia and Leonard Woolf visit Bowen's Court.

1935 *The House in Paris*. Cameron appointed to the BBC and he and Bowen move to Clarence Terrace, Regent's Park, London.

1936 Goronwy Rees, on the fringes of the Cambridge spy circle and romantically involved with Bowen, falls in love with Rosamond Lehmann at a summer house party at Bowen's Court. He is thought to be the model for Eddie in *The Death of the Heart*.

1937 Member of the Irish Academy of Letters. Begins affairs with Sean O'Faoláin, who fosters her understanding of Irish nationalism and Irish literary culture, and, briefly, with May Sarton, with whom she stays friendly until the 1950s before abruptly dropping her.

1938 *The Death of the Heart*. In the summer in Ireland she meets, separately, W. B. Yeats and Frank O'Connor.

1939 Bowen is guest of honour at the fifth annual banquet of the Irish Women Writers' Club in Dublin in June. After the outbreak of the Second World War, Bowen decides to stay in London where she works as an ARP warden.

1940 Offers her services to the British Ministry of Information, which commissions her to write confidential reports on conditions in neutral Ireland, necessitating several wartime trips back to Ireland. When published, these reports would damage her reputation in Ireland. She discusses this mission with Virginia Woolf in July during a walk through London.

1941 *Look at All Those Roses*. Bowen visits Woolf at Rodmell, shortly before the latter's death. Begins affair with Charles Ritchie, a Canadian diplomat. Their relationship will survive Ritchie's marriage in 1948 and several changes of country.

1942 *Bowen's Court. Seven Winters: Memories of a Dublin Childhood. English Novelists*.

1944 Bowen's Regent's Park home bombed in July, obliging Bowen and her husband to move out until October.
1945 *The Demon Lover and Other Stories*.
1946 Appointed *Cork Examiner*'s accredited correspondent for the Paris Peace Conference which Ritchie also attended.
1948 Awarded the CBE. In early February, Bowen embarks on a lecture tour for the British Council to Czechoslovakia and Austria, speaking on the novel and the short story. Such tours to Central Europe become a regular feature of her life in the 1950s. In late February, *Castle Anna*, a play co-written with John Parry, is put on at the Lyric Theatre, Hammersmith. 1948–50, she is acting principal of Kent Education Committee's summer school for English teachers at Folkestone.
1949 *The Heat of the Day*. Honorary DLitt from Trinity College, Dublin. Member of the Royal Commission on Capital Punishment which reported in 1953 in favour of abolition. First meeting with Eudora Welty, with whom she was to be close friends.
1950 *Collected Impressions*. Bowen intensifies her magazine writing, journalism, broadcasting, and lecturing in American universities, in order to pay for the upkeep of Bowen's Court. She now spends part of every year in America.
1951 *The Shelbourne*. Eudora Welty stays at Bowen's Court working on 'The Bride of the Innisfallen'.
1952 Due to financial difficulties and Alan's ill health they give up their Regent's Park home and move to Bowen's Court where, in August, Alan dies.
1955 *A World of Love*.
1956 Honorary DLitt from Oxford University.
1958 Writes to Charles Ritchie in June asking him to send her a cheque for a hundred dollars. A later letter from Rome announces her decision to sell Bowen's Court.

1959 From October 1959 to January 1960 does another spell as writer in residence at the American Academy in Rome. December 1959 sells Bowen's Court to a neighbouring farmer, Cornelius O'Keefe. From now until the end of 1960 she is in effect homeless and in some mental and physical distress.

1960 *A Time in Rome*. In April there is a two-day auction of the contents of Bowen's Court. By the end of the summer the house has been demolished. In November, with friends' help, she moves to a flat in Oxford owned by Isaiah Berlin.

1961 Writes script for CBS documentary on Ireland, 'The Tear and the Smile'.

1962 *Afterthought: Pieces About Writing*.

1964 *The Little Girls*. Spends Christmas, as often, in Ireland with the Vernons and sees her collaborative project, 'A Nativity Play', performed in the Catholic Cathedral in Limerick. It will be performed again in the Protestant Cathedral in Derry in 1970 as an ecumenical event.

1965 *A Day in the Dark and Other Stories*. *The Good Tiger* (children's book). Made Companion of Literature. In March moves into a small house in Hythe where she had lived as a child with her mother, calling it Carbery after her maternal family's estate in Ireland.

1966 Her script for 'Kinsale, Son et Lumière' is performed on 22 May as part of the local arts festival.

1968 *Eva Trout, or Changing Scenes*.

1969 Teaches on the Creative Writing programme at Princeton. At the end of the year visits Eudora Welty in Jackson, Mississippi.

1970 On one of her regular trips back to Ireland revisits the site of Bowen's Court. Ritchie's diary records her contemplating a move to Clontarf, Dublin.

1973 Dies of lung cancer in University College Hospital, London, on 22 February, with her cousin Audrey and

Charles Ritchie by her side. Buried as 'Mrs Cameron' in St Colman's churchyard beside Bowen's Court.

1975 *Pictures and Conversations* (essays, fragments of memoir and an unfinished novel).

Note: The dates given are for the earliest publication of a Bowen work, whether in the UK or America.

INTRODUCTION
Reading Elizabeth Bowen

Elizabeth Bowen (1899–1973) is now recognized as one of the finest twentieth-century novelists and short story writers to come out of Ireland, her work featuring alongside that of James Joyce and Samuel Beckett (Corcoran 2004, Mooney 2009, Pearson 2015). Her wild, unsettling imagination, her wit and talent for precise social observation, as well as her unnerving insight into the treachery of memory and the uncanniness, dislocations and even traumas lying beneath the surface of everyday life, make up just some of her gifts as a writer. Added to these, her grasp of history and the wider ramifications of the major political upheavals of her lifetime – the First World War, the Irish War of Independence, the Second World War, America's growing postwar influence – proclaim her a major writer in the English language.

This has not always been the case. Although Bowen was a noted literary figure in her lifetime, after her death critical opinion tended to downplay her achievements. Scholars overlooked the extraordinary reach and startling strangeness of her vision and style. Instead, consciously or unconsciously focusing on stereotypes of gender, class and ethnicity, they confined her work to such limiting categories as middlebrow novelist, Big House author, inheritor of Bloomsbury, women's writer, and novelist of manners. Victoria Glendinning's 1977 biography and Hermione Lee's 1981 critical study together with Lee's 1986 selection of Bowen's prose, *The Mulberry Tree*, went some way to reviving Bowen's reputation. Masculinist definitions of modernism, however, as well as certain strands of Irish literary nationalism, still tended to exclude her work from proper consideration.

The development of Irish Studies led to Bowen's complex and divided Anglo-Irish identity being written back into the Irish canon in the 1990s in studies by Roy Foster (1993), Declan Kiberd (1996) and Vera Kreilkamp (1998). In these readings, the radical instability of home, personal identity and language in her work is traced back to the dispossessed and uncertain position of the Anglo-Irish in the newly-independent Irish state, and her 1929 novel *The Last September* is acknowledged as a crucial text. W. J. McCormack (1993) identified Bowen as an inheritor of the Irish Protestant Gothic literary tradition reinventing it, notably in her wartime fiction, for her modernist explorations of extreme psychic states. Margot Gayle Backus (1999) introduced a gender dimension into postcolonial analysis of the Anglo-Irish Bowen, while Neil Corcoran (2004), bringing together Bowen's Anglo-Irish context and her late modernism, paid attention to the complexities of Bowen's style and literary inheritance. Nels Pearson's (2015) placing of her beside Joyce and Beckett as an Irish cosmopolitan, that is, with unresolved and conflicted roots in Ireland but looking beyond that country to international settings and a wider, European cultural dispossession, was a welcome opening out of the topic of Bowen's Irishness.

Feminist and gender studies provided another route into her work, emphasizing the way in which Bowen complicates her critique of the Anglo-Irish by her attention to questions of gender and sexuality. Ann Owens Weekes (1990) placed Bowen in a tradition of Irish women's writing, as did the discussion of the conflict between nation and gender in Bowen and other Irish women writers in my own *Twentieth-Century Fiction by Irish Women: Nation and Gender* (2007). Several essays in the collection *Elizabeth Bowen* (2009), edited by Eibhear Walshe and published in a series titled *Irish Writers in their Time*, drew on feminist and queer theory while keeping Bowen's Irish context firmly in mind.

Feminist studies outside the field of Irish Studies focused on the emotional upheavals and displacements in Bowen's personal life as reflected in her writing. In her short study, *Elizabeth Bowen* (1990), Phyllis Lassner applied psychoanalytical and feminist theories to Bowen's presentation of female sexuality and the relationships between women and between mothers and children. In *Elizabeth Bowen: A Reputation in Writing* (1994), Renée Hoogland gave a controversial lesbian reading of her work, which was later refined and expanded on by such scholars as Patricia Coughlan (1997, 2009) and Tina O'Toole (2011).

By the 1990s Bowen studies had taken off, but at this stage Bowen might have found difficulty recognizing herself. National identity was always fraught for her. Though her family's roots in Ireland went back to the seventeenth century and she spent large parts of her life in that country, as an Anglo-Irishwoman her relationship with Ireland was conflicted. At times, particularly when addressing an Irish audience, as during the banquet given in her honour in Dublin by the Irish Women Writers' Club in June 1939, she proclaimed her Irish identity (*Irish Independent*, 8 June 1939: 10). In an interview for *The Bell* in 1942 she explained:

> I regard myself as an Irish novelist. As long as I can remember, I've been extremely conscious of being Irish – even when I was writing about very un-Irish things such as suburban life in Paris or the English seaside (Foster, 1995: 118).

At other periods, notably during the later stages of the Second World War, when she came to resent Ireland's neutrality, and in her final years after the sale of Bowen's Court, momentary exasperation against Ireland tipped over into expressions of loathing (Lee 1999: 7). Yet, according to Charles Ritchie's diary, towards the end of her life she was contemplating moving back to Ireland, a move that might well have taken place had not her final illness intervened (*LCW*: 463).

Bowen's attitude to feminism was scarcely less conflicted. She disliked the overt feminism in her friend Virginia Woolf's work describing it as 'a bleak quality, an aggressive streak, which can but irritate' (*CI*: 81). 'I am not, and never shall be, a feminist' she declared (*PPT*: 377), although, like Mrs Kerr in *The Hotel*, she might have added: 'but I do like being a woman' (*H*: 11). Bowen's interpretation of feminism was that it implicitly or explicitly denigrated men's achievements and this she did not wish to do. She did not on that account think that women were lesser beings, only that their particular talents often suffered from being corralled into masculinised professions, and she resisted the label feminist because she felt it denied the importance to domestic and social life of the non-professional woman. In an interview for the BBC, broadcast in 1941, she insisted on women's gifts: 'Flexibility, quickness in the uptake, sensitiveness and a sympathetic attitude towards the other person's point of view' (*LI*: 288).

Bowen's support for the homemaking capacities of women co-existed, however, with her public life as a professional writer, journalist, broadcaster, reviewer, her war work and her service on the Royal Commission on Capital Punishment. In addition, as Geneviève Brassard has observed, throughout her fiction Bowen makes 'narrative interventions that look and sound feminist' (Brassard, 2007: 286). In her review of *The Daughters of Erin* by Elizabeth Coxhead, Bowen addressed herself particularly to Irish women, urging them to look to the examples of Maud Gonne, Constance Markievicz, Sarah Purser, Sarah Allgood and Máire O'Neill, in order to break through into the arts, theatre, and politics (*LI*: 130–2).

Despite her life as a professional in the public eye, Bowen found widowhood, without her husband's practical business sense to rely on, very difficult, almost unnatural, admitting in a letter to her lover, Charles Ritchie:

> I sometimes wonder whether even *you*, knowing me as well

as you do, really realize my horror of my state as a *femme seule* (legal definition). It seems to me abnormal, it fills me with a sense of ghastly injury, that I should have to organize my own life. It seems abnormal that any woman should have to do so (*LCW*: 350).

At the same time, she insisted to her first lover, Humphry House, that she was a writer before she was a woman (Laurence, 2019: 136).

Bowen's attitude to the 'woman' question, like her attitude to Ireland, was never straightforward. Her work adopts a consistently sceptical position on heterosexual romance and she herself did not lead a conventional married life, conducting several lengthy relationships with male lovers and at least one lesbian affair (with May Sarton when staying at her house in Rye in 1937). Though she is known to have rejected advances from Nancy Spain and Carson McCullers, the possibility of other lesbian affairs remains. Certainly the bonds between women in her work are strong. Male homosexuality, largely veiled until her final novel, also features throughout Bowen's fiction and in a rich reading of the early novels, Elizabeth Cullingford linked the presentation of the only child, a theme with Anglo-Irish resonances (*BC*: 20), to Bowen's portrayal of queerness and mobile gender identities (Cullingford, 2007: 276–305). The instability of sexual desire in her fiction and her reluctance to pin down and label sexual identities make Bowen peculiarly relevant to our times.

Bowen might have been happier to claim an identity as a war writer for she recognized that the Second World War was a time when she came into her own both in her personal life, through meeting Charles Ritchie, and as a writer who was to produce some of the finest fiction to come out of the war. Scholars such as Heather Bryant Jordan (1992), Gill Plain (1996) and Clair Wills (2007) point out that the themes of surveillance, treachery, and divided allegiance felt by Bowen as a member of the Anglo-Irish, 'potted at by the Irish and sold out by the British' (*LCW*: 54), and in her personal life as a result of her affair with Ritchie, were accentuated by her experience of the fetid atmosphere of wartime London, by her sense of the claustrophobia and stagnation in Irish life resulting from Ireland's policy of neutrality, and by her own role in writing secret reports on the situation in neutral Ireland for the British Ministry of Information.

The atmosphere of treachery and guilt in Bowen's war novel, *The Heat of the Day* (1949), led Allan Hepburn (2009) to add Bowen to Kristin Bluemel's category of intermodernists. In Bluemel's formulation, intermodernists are writers from the 1930s, 40s and early 50s, geographical outsiders and often dismissed as middlebrows, yet whose work straddles the divide between lowbrow and highbrow, between commercial and experimental, and has the potential to be reinterpreted in radical ways (Bluemel, 2009). This political Bowen, eliminating once and for all the description 'lady of letters' that also bedeviled Woolf, is now available to scholars through Hepburn's edited collections of her essays, broadcasts, speeches and interviews (2008, 2010), complemented by Eibhear Walshe's 2011 anthology of her non-fiction writing on Irish topics, including her wartime reports on Irish neutrality. Despite the domestic settings, Bowen's fiction regularly indicates a wider cultural and political context. 'Domestic crisis only becomes important where there is a lively sense of what lies beyond its stage', she argued in 'What We Need in Writing' (1936) (*PPT*: 309).

The fact is that, given the many different genres in which Bowen wrote – Gothic and sensation fiction, romance, comedy of manners, domestic fiction, thriller, horror – adapting each to recurring Bowen obsessions, her work fits uneasily into any single category. Her unpredictability as a writer and the sheer breadth of her vision make it risky to impose any fixed ideological reading on her work. The most innovative critical readings of recent times have opened up the ambiguities, mobile sexual desires and traumas in her writing in order to explore the interweaving of personal and political ruptures in her life. Arguing that traditional concepts of realism are inappropriate for Bowen's fiction, in their 1994 study, *Elizabeth Bowen and the Dissolution of the Novel: Still Lives*, Andrew Bennett and Nicholas Royle made use of post-Derridean critical language to discuss states of abeyances, catatonia, dreams, hauntings and instabilities in her work, providing what was at that point a very much less familiar Bowen. Maud Ellmann's 2003 *Elizabeth Bowen: The Shadow Across the Page* employed psychoanalytical and deconstructive methods to illuminate connections between Bowen's life and her writing, between Irish and modernist traditions, and the recurrence of erotic triangles in her work. Bowen's personal fascination with ghosts and the uncanny was highlighted as Ellmann expanded on the unnerving effect of Bowen's hallucinatory treatment of objects, explored by Jacqueline Rose (2000) and later taken up by Elizabeth Inglesby (2007) in her discussion of Bowen's literary animism. Such readings led to a welcome revaluation of Bowen's often neglected later novels which gained fuller meaning through these studies.

The religious and conservative Bowen at the heart of John Coates' *Social Discontinuity in the Novels of Elizabeth Bowen: The Conservative Quest* (1998) provided a counter to such readings and, though Coates' study has been sidelined in subsequent Bowen criticism, it is worth pausing for a moment to consider this aspect of Bowen's life, underlined by Rosamond Lehmann in her obituary for her friend: 'It is not generally realized how firmly and deeply based was her Christian faith' (*WL*: 7). Bowen's Christian beliefs, never worn on her sleeve, run underground through her fiction, and her letters to Ritchie contain many references to church attendance both in Ireland and England, casually cite Biblical quotations and often mention prayer. It might be argued that church going was expected behaviour in Bowen's lifetime; certainly her description of being taken as a child to Protestant churches in Dublin and Farahy suggests a tribal element. Later, though surrounded by sceptics and atheists and moving in generally secular circles, she continued to attend church services throughout her adult life, which suggests something beyond custom (Laurence, 2019: 65).

According to Bowen's first biographer: 'Her Anglicanism was more than merely social. She had a real knowledge of her Church's liturgy and a respect for its traditions' (Glendinning, 1978: 294). In the late 1960s, when the Alternative Service was introduced, Bowen's opposition to it was strong enough to cause her to leave her local church in Hythe for one where the 1662 Communion service was still followed. Ritchie, with whom Bowen sometimes shared her church-going, attests in his diary to her belief in an afterlife (*LCW*: 468) and she received holy communion in hospital during her final days. 'I cannot claim to believe in *un*intelligent faith' says the mild clergyman in 'The Last Bus' (*B*: 273). In the light of recent studies of Christian motifs and spiritual themes in modernist writers by, for example, Pericles Lewis (2010), Lara Vetter (2010), Suzanne Hobson (2011) and Jane de Gay (2018), 'intelligent faith' in Bowen's work deserves closer inspection and will be touched on in this study.

As Bowen's reputation became more firmly established at the centre of the canon of twentieth-century literature, monographs and articles written from various critical perspectives began to appear more regularly. Bowen's final four novels were the particular focus of Lis Christensen's 2001 study, while Nicola Darwood (2012) discussed the transition from innocence to experience as a necessary part of Bowen's characters' epistemological journey and Jessica Gildersleeve (2014) explored the theme of trauma in Bowen's fiction through the lens of deconstructive and psychoanalytical theories. In 2018, the inauguration of the online *Elizabeth Bowen Review* provided a welcome space for scholars to open up new lines of enquiry, pursuing such topics as fairytales, the phenomenological body, and the adaptation of Futurist techniques in Bowen's work. In 2019, contributors to *Elizabeth*

Bowen: Theory, Thought and Things edited by Jessica Gildersleeve and Patricia Juliana Smith, explored Bowen's narrative techniques from a range of innovative theoretical angles, contributing to our understanding of Bowen as a sophisticated intellectual deeply engaged with the literary, social and artistic life of her time. In 2019 also, Victoria Glendinning's 1977 biography was supplemented by Patricia Laurence's up-dated account which is more in tune with recent Bowen scholarship.

Given the plethora of detailed scholarly studies of Bowen's work in recent years, a short, up-to date and accessible introduction providing an overview of different approaches to her writing and suggesting possibilities for future research seems timely. Beyond this, given the title of the series to which this book belongs, it is proposed to study Irishness as a particular strand running through and uniting her work, building on the observations of scholars such as Heather Laird, Julie Anne Stevens, Vera Kreilkamp and Patricia Coughlan who have argued that Ireland permeates, not just Bowen's Irish-set fiction but all of her work, something that is borne out by Bowen's own comment on origins in her unfinished, posthumously-published memoir, *Pictures and Conversations*: 'My own: Anglo-Ireland and its peculiarities. The infiltration – I believe? – of at least some of these peculiarities into my books' (*MT*: 297).

The political situation of the Anglo-Irish is arguably the impetus behind themes that link Bowen's Irish novels with those set elsewhere, themes such as fantasy colliding with reality, intergenerational conflict, only children, dispossession, uncertain identity, treachery, haunting by the past, and the pivotal role of the First World War. Bowen herself believed her work had been influenced by a specifically Anglo-Irish bravado employed to conceal insecurity and even trauma (*MT*: 276). Laird (2009) argues that one of the threads connecting the Anglo-Irish Bowen with the Bowen who dissected English society is her attention to moments when the pose breaks down, the mask slips, and the pressures such facades seek to contain are glimpsed beneath the surface. In an interview broadcast in 1950, Bowen explained: 'the more the surface seems to heave or threaten to crack the more its actual pattern fascinates me. What do I mean by the surface? Civilisation, any kind of control' (*LI*: 283). In a letter to Ritchie, Bowen identified a moment when one such fracture occurred, namely the episode of the insults, banging on the table and throwing of shoes by the Russian delegation at a UN meeting in 1960 which Ritchie attended:

> Things like that must be like the whole surface of life cracking. I mean, it's the sort of thing one never expected to live to see ... I think the horror is, the sense of fumes of evil when people lose control (*LCW*: 360).

The theme of 'the whole surface of life cracking' had a personal resonance for Bowen. Her Anglo-Irish background, a class that had 'made an art of maintaining its position *in vacuo*' (*LCW*: 54), created in her a preternatural awareness of the precarious political structures on which lives are based. As a child witnessing her father's descent into insanity, she had experienced her apparently happy family life shattered by another sighting of the void (Laurence, 2019: 16–18). In *Pictures and Conversations* she glosses over this period, stating that she came out of it with nothing worse than a stammer. Nevertheless the stammer was to be lifelong and severe, and a glimpse of what was surely a traumatic episode for a young child emerges in her description of 'the tensions and mystery of my father's illness, the apprehensive silences or chaotic shoutings' (*MT*: 270).

In addition to her father's insanity and her consequent uprooting from Ireland, the death of her mother when she was thirteen led to her being parceled out in her teenage years among various relatives. Such experience resulted in a proliferation of orphans and refugees in her work, and Phyllis Lassner and Paula

Derdiger (2009) have explored the figure of the dispossessed other in Bowen's writing. While bearing in mind that to confine Bowen's writing to a single ideological lens is to impoverish it, it will be one of the aims of this short study to highlight those moments when cataclysms occur in a body of work that, in Anne Wyatt-Brown's memorable phrase, 'juxtaposes the asocial and psychotic with the everyday and the ordinary' (Wyatt-Brown, 1993: 165).

CHAPTER ONE

The Female *Bildungsroman*: *The Hotel* and *The Last September*

The Hotel (1927)

Elizabeth Bowen's first published novel, *The Hotel* (1927), opens on one of those moments when the veneer of civilized life among the upper-middle classes appears to crack. Miss Fitzgerald has quarreled so violently with her friend, Miss Pym, that after storming out of the eponymous hotel in Italy, she stands paralysed in the middle of the road, 'frightened by an interior quietness and by the thought that she had for once in her life stopped thinking and might never begin again' (*H*: 5). Notwithstanding Bowen's expressed dislike of categorizing people's emotional lives (*LCW*: 417), there is scope here for reading *The Hotel*, as Layla Ferrández Melero has, as a lesbian novel (Melero, 2019: 71–84). Characteristically Bowen leaves the relationship between the two women undefined, the women being described simply as 'friends'. Nevertheless their relationship is sufficiently close for the world of both women to have been turned upside down by this sudden, violent explosion of 'bitterness' on Miss Fitzgerald's part.

Fitzgerald is an Irish name (the Fitzgeralds, like the Bowens, came over to Ireland from Wales), whereas Pym is solidly Anglo-Saxon. Given that Bowen, even in her most domestic passages, always had an eye to the wider political context, it may be permissible to read into this scene a veiled reference to recent events in Ireland. Miss Pym, the Englishwoman, is surprised by her companion's violent outburst. 'Who would ever have thought the Irish would turn out so disloyal?' an English army wife will remark in Bowen's next novel (*LS*: 46). Meanwhile Miss Fitzgerald, 'having discharged with such bitterness of finality that last shot in her locker' (*H*: 5), takes to the hills like an Irish rebel. Later, as Miss Pym walks down to the tennis courts with Mrs Kerr, she is suddenly confronted by her erstwhile friend and wonders: 'Had they walked into an ambush?' (*H*: 7). Miss Pym feels that in that moment of quarrel 'they had seen each other crudely illuminated' (*H*: 8). 'Illumination' in Bowen's work is a word often associated with war: in her short story, 'Summer Night', set during the Second World War, Justin will refer to the war as 'an awful illumination' (*CS*: 590). The personal world of the two women has been shaken in a way that reveals a vacuum beneath:

> They had had, at that moment when everything tottered, worse than a sense of destruction: they had felt the whole force of a doubt in that moment: had there ever been *anything* there? (*H*: 8).

In *The Last September*, Hugo Montmorency will extend similar doubts into the political arena, describing the Anglo-Irish as 'rather scared, rather isolated, not expressing anything except tenacity to something that isn't there – that never was there' (*LS*: 82). Bowen's acute awareness of the precariousness of her own class in the newly independent Irish nation lies behind her portrayal of the unease beneath the apparent complacencies of the upper middle classes in *The Hotel*. Later in the novel Miss Pym, in a crisis of confidence triggered by the outing to a villa abandoned by its White Russian owners since the Russian revolution, will question the point of the upper classes (*H*: 106).

In an interview for *The Bell*, Bowen suggested that an Irish sensibility colours even her works set outside Ireland (Foster, 1995: 118), and this opening scene of her first novel indicates that attention to Bowen's Irishness adds layers of meaning even to action not set in Ireland. The shattering quarrel between Miss Fitzgerald and Miss Pym is recalled at the conclusion of *The Hotel* but now the two women sit 'hand in hand, reunited, in perfect security' (*H*: 175), a sign not only of the priority given in this novel to female friendship/lesbian romance over the heterosexual marriage plot but also perhaps of Bowen's hopes for the future relationship between the two countries which, given the hyphenated nature of her own Anglo-Irish identity, she was always wishing could be closer.

Irish resonances may frame *The Hotel* but what the novel's first readers saw in it was a comedy of manners depicting the eccentricities of the English abroad in the style of Henry James, E. M. Forster and Virginia Woolf (of *The Voyage Out*). In a letter to Charles Ritchie, Bowen pinpointed Proust's Balbec hotel scenes from *À l'Ombre de Jeunes Filles en Fleur* as a seminal influence, together with her memories of a tedious winter spent at an 'appalling hotel at Bordighera' with the Colleys in 1921 during which time she broke off her engagement to an English army officer: 'I expect I *was* in ways rather like Sydney' (*LCW*: 140). For *The Hotel* is also a female *Bildungsroman* centred on twenty-two-year-old Sydney who, having teetered on the edge of a breakdown through overwork (echoes here of Bowen's father), is spending the winter in Italy with her aunt.

Sydney's name reflects the vogue for androgynous names given to the more independent young protagonists in interwar women's writing, notably in the work of Bowen's early mentor, Rose Macaulay, as they grapple with the problem of attaining adult identity in a society that offers few opportunities for women. None of the married women's lives Sydney observes in the hotel seem to her appealing. Neither Mrs Duperrier anguished by, but turning a blind eye to, her husband's self-deceiving propensity for the company of young women, nor Mrs Lee-Mittison endeavouring to make a home for her husband in a succession of hotel rooms, provide satisfactory role models: 'It seemed odder than ever to Sydney, eyeing these couples, that men and women should be expected to pair off for life' (*H*: 18).

Inaugurating a series of youthful characters in Bowen's work susceptible to revolutionary fantasies, Sydney pictures a sudden invasion of Saracens descending on the hotel's too complacent inhabitants, anticipating the scene in *The Last September* where Lois, more realistically, imagines Danielstown in flames:

> 'Wouldn't it be nice', she said, suddenly smiling, 'if the Saracens were to appear on the skyline, land, and ravage the Hotel? They all take it for granted – down there – that there aren't any more Saracens' (*H*: 35).

First in a line of 'Bowen's young women' who look to older, more powerful women for help in establishing their adult identity in a masculinist society, Sydney seeks from Mrs Kerr a clue as to how to live a woman's life while avoiding the stereotypes of wife and mother. Lacking a mother and father, Sydney needs her identity to be mirrored back in Mrs Kerr's maternal gaze, for only then will she exist as a person:

> It became no longer a question of – What did Mrs Kerr think of her? – but rather – Did Mrs Kerr ever think of her? The possibility of not being kept in mind seemed to Sydney at that moment a kind of extinction (*H*: 14).

Ironically it is because Mrs Kerr escapes feminine stereotypes that she is unable to provide the validating reflection Sydney needs.

Mrs Kerr is a widow, but apparently an unmourning one, for her behaviour is confused with that of a divorcée (*H*: 54). She participates in none of the activities expected of her and makes the experienced matrons in the drawing room uneasy: 'One is never comfortable in talking to her' (*H*: 52). Though she cannot put this into words, Sydney suspects some 'falsity; an imposture' (*H*: 63) in Mrs Kerr's new-found maternal feeling towards Ronald and in fact her motherhood *is* fake since she responds to her son's obvious desire for a home by asking: 'How long is it, I wonder, since you and I have kept house? Perhaps I have deprived you of something? – I cannot feel that I have' (*H*: 95). She soon tires of his company: 'She tugged gently at a fold of her tea-gown on which he happened to be sitting and swept him away from her with a gesture' (*H*: 166). Mrs Kerr uses Ronald as a defence against Sydney's demands for intimacy, deliberately humiliating the girl by flaunting her motherhood while simultaneously, as Elizabeth Cullingford notes, martyrizing her son who fails to progress beyond the Oedipal stage in his relationship with his mother (Cullingford, 2007: 276–305).

Sydney's growth to adulthood proceeds by way of a series of betrayals on Mrs Kerr's part leading up to the scene in the café where Mrs Kerr subtly but cruelly indicates that Sydney expected more from the relationship than she has ever been prepared to give. Here betrayal, which in *The Last September* will take on a specifically political resonance, is personal. Sydney is left paralysed on the curbstone by the chasm Mrs Kerr's cruelty has suddenly opened up in her life, recalling Miss Fitzgerald's immobility in the opening scene after her shattering quarrel with Miss Pym.

Dropped by Mrs Kerr, Sydney finds solace with James Milton, a clergyman who, despite his surname, wears his faith lightly but exudes an air of middle-aged solidity. The novel is clear about the cultural pressures on young women to marry suitably and produce children: any personal desires they may have must be sacrificed in order to maintain the continuity of the tribe. Sydney has a personal distaste for procreation: '"What a lot of energy is wasted" she observed, "in replacing one lot of people by another exactly the same"' (*H*: 141). Sydney's statement is the prelude to a series of anxieties around reproduction, miscarriages and infertility that will reverberate through Bowen's work. Society consuming the lives of the young is a theme Bowen will return to in *The Last*

September where it is placed in the specific context of Anglo-Ireland and 'colonialism as a pervasive historical system that appropriates the sexuality and lives of Anglo-Irish children' (Backus, 1999: 8).

Here, the residents of the hotel automatically assume that Sydney will abandon her medical studies on marriage so that, engaged to Milton, Sydney comes to feel she has been written into a text over which she has no control:

> She stood between Tessa and Mrs Kerr as inanimate and objective as a young girl in a story told by a man, incapable of a thought or a feeling that was not attributed to her (*H*: 156).

The experience of being a passenger in a speeding car that nearly goes over the edge of a precipice jolts Sydney out of her passivity, shocking her into an awareness of mortality that is a turning point for her: 'I had had no idea we were as real as this. I'd never realized it mattered so much', she explains to Milton as she breaks off their engagement (*H*: 160).

The Hotel is a comedy of manners tinged with modernist awareness that life had changed fundamentally as a result of the First World War, unravelling Edwardian certainties, disrupting the marriage plot, and irretrievably altering the relationship between the sexes (Bennett, 2009: 29–30). Virginia Woolf, later Bowen's friend, captured this postwar sense of living and writing in a transformed world:

> We are sharply cut off from our predecessors. A shift in the scale – the war, the sudden slip of masses held in position for ages – has shaken the fabric from top to bottom, alienated us from the past and made us perhaps too vividly conscious of the present. Every day we find ourselves doing, saying, or thinking things that would have been impossible to our fathers (Woolf, 1994: 238).

In the aftermath of the cataclysmic war, young women like Sydney found the scripts for their lives dispiriting. Even the Lawrence girls, on the look-out for husbands, feel that young men nowadays are not really worth the effort and that in any case, as a result of the war, there are too few of them around. One of the few eligible young men in the hotel is the ironically named Victor Ammering, casualty of the war, and 'said to be suffering from nervous depression as a consequence' (*H*: 19). This was a condition Bowen was familiar with from her period working in a hospital for shell-shocked soldiers (Ellmann, 2004: 56–7). He and Veronica Lawrence become engaged in a provisional, desultory way, very different from the passionate romance plot of the Victorian novel.

Europe's interwar paralysis is comically underlined in the scene where the hotel lift becomes suspended between floors and Joan Lawrence even suggests, perceptively, that the period they are living through may be merely a pause between wars (*H*: 49). Ronald's distress about the economic situation in Germany underlines this prophetic observation (*H:* 94), while a visit to a villa, owned by Russians but deserted since the Bolshevik Revolution, references another recent political trauma. Modernist dislocation is emphasized by the hotel setting which underlines the transient lives of its residents. Ronald, as a result of his mother's repudiation of motherhood, has no home, and neither have the Lee-Mattisons who, like the Anglo-Irish Montmorencys in *The Last September*, intersperse life in hotel rooms with visits to friends. Homelessness had an intensely personal resonance for Bowen who, between her mother's death in 1912 and her marriage to Alan Cameron in 1923, essentially resided in other people's houses. Only on marriage did she regain a permanent home: 'I was now located, the mistress of a house; and the sensation of *living* anywhere, as apart from paying a succession of visits, was new to me' (Glendinning, 1978: 61).

Many elements of Bowen's fiction are already present in this first novel: a young woman uncertain of her future, a precocious child (Cordelia) who sees through the civilised façade so carefully maintained by her elders, a powerful older woman, the displaced and the homeless. The novel resists the romance plot and disrupts readers' expectations of closure as Sydney's future remains undecided and the hotel guests disperse in disorderly fashion. Female friendship remains but even that is presented as fragile: another quarrel between Miss Fitzgerald and Miss Pym is only narrowly averted.

The dislocations and the fragmented ending are characteristic of emerging modernist fiction but also, as Vera Kreilkamp argues, the result of Bowen's Anglo-Irish perception of the fragility of social structures:

> The strikingly modernist sense of psychic incoherence and homelessness shaping Bowen's fiction stemmed no less from an Irish Ascendancy sensibility than from her receptivity to twentieth-century cultural innovation (Kreilkamp, 2009: 13).

Bowen herself pinpointed an 'acceptance of more or less permanent insecurity as a basis for life' as an Anglo-Irish trait (*SIW*: 234). It is to that Anglo-Ireland we now turn.

The Last September (1929)

In *The Hotel* the English visitors are outsiders, in temporary possession of the hotel, and surrounded by largely invisible Italians. In *The Last September* (1929), the female *Bildungsroman* takes place in Danielstown, an Irish Big House owned by the Anglo-Irish Naylor family, but one whose ownership during the War of Independence, defended by the British army, watched over by Irish gunmen concealed in the hills, is becoming increasingly precarious. The novel opens in September 1920, the year before the Anglo-Irish, always colonial outsiders in Ireland, had their dispossession confirmed by the treaty of Irish independence which left them without a political identity. It is, as Bowen explained in her preface to the second American edition of *The Last September*, 'fiction with the texture of history' (*MT*: 125).

Big Houses like Danielstown, the 'big' referring to social significance as much as to size, flourished in Ireland during the eighteenth century when the Protestant Ascendancy asserted its political and economic power over the lives of its dispossessed Catholic tenants. The Big House influence peaked in the latter part of the eighteenth century under Grattan's Parliament. The dissolution of this Parliament under the terms of the 1801 Act of Union rendered the Anglo-Irish politically and socially irrelevant. Evictions, tenant poverty and the devastating mid-nineteenth-century famines hardened Irish resentment towards the Big House. A series of land reforms from the 1880s onwards, culminating in the 1903 Wyndham Land Act, deprived Anglo-Irish landlords of their rental properties and left them struggling to maintain their houses and demesnes. In *The Last September* Bowen, a thwarted architect (*LI*: 330), portrays the burden of the Big House on its twentieth-century inheritors through the architecture of Danielstown. Danielstown's vast façade, high ceilings, and walls crowded with ancestors' portraits dwarf its current inhabitants and impede conversation.

From the outset Anglo-Irish fiction, depicting the lives of colonizing landlords in their Big Houses, inevitably incorporated a political and historical dimension as, in the hands of writers like Maria Edgeworth, Charles Maturin, Sheridan Le Fanu, and Somerville and Ross, the genre revealed the slowly unraveling status of the Anglo-Irish. Characteristic features of this Big House fiction included a decaying country house, tensions between its irresponsible inhabitants and their Catholic tenants, a declining family line, lingering guilt over the original sin of colonial misappropriation leading to anxieties of ownership, and an outsider, such as a Catholic land agent or a rising professional man, who infiltrates the Big House with a view to taking it over (Kreilkamp, 1998: 21–2). Not all of these characteristics are present in *The Last September* where attention to gender, through the portrayal of nineteen-year-old Lois Farquar's *Bildung*, provides another dimension to the Big House novel.

The Anglo-Irish Naylors are uncomfortably situated between their traditional ties to Britain where, in Bowen's words, 'their sons were schooled, in whose wars their sons had for generations fought, and to which they owed their "Ascendancy" lands and power' (*MT*: 125), and affection for their Irish tenants forged through the bonds of daily life. Silence is an essential tool for survival as their world collapses around them, for there is no guarantee that in the end they will be supported either by the British or by the Irish. An evocative description of Danielstown seen through Lois' eyes after meeting one of the Naylors' tenants whose son is fighting for Irish independence underlines, by means of Bowen's characteristic literary animism, that, no longer the confident symbol of eighteenth-century landlordism, the Big House is, in 1920, fearful of its status in Irish countryside:

> The house seemed to be pressing down low in apprehension, hiding its face, as though it had her vision of where it was. It seemed to gather its trees close in fright and amazement at the wide, light, lovely unloving country, the unwilling bosom whereon it was set (*LS*: 66).

In her ground-breaking essay on affinities between Bowen and that other Irish Protestant, Samuel Beckett, Sinéad Mooney observes: 'the characters in *The Last September* are half-conscious that they are in an endgame, caught in a running-down or diminishing cycle' (Mooney, 2009: 20). Any moments of awareness of their situation, described by Bowen as 'more nearly heart-breaking than they cared to show' (*MT*: 125), occur in momentary asides such as Lady Naylor's observation on pre-revolutionary Russia – 'I can't think how any of those Tsars had any confidence' (*LS*: 135) – referencing, as in *The Hotel*, wider political dispossession.

Since for much of the novel the denizens of Danielstown adopt a self-protective policy of not acknowledging the ambushes, arrests and raids going on around them, the major crack, or sudden violent eruption that reveals the abyss beneath, does not occur until Chapter Fifteen, during the encounter at the mill between inhabitants of the Big House and an IRA gunman, which obliges Lois, at least, to face up to the reality of her situation.

Margot Gayle Backus has explored the silences that Anglo-Irish offspring were trained to maintain over anything that might challenge the legitimacy of the colonialists' version of Irish history (Backus, 1999). Both in *The Last September* and in her family memoir, *Bowen's Court* (1942), Bowen breaks that silence and in 1952 she stated very clearly:

> In the Anglo-Irish, those invaders and settlers who came to conquer, stayed to possess and love, national responsibility did come to be born, but social responsibility, alas, not. Where there was benevolence, there should have been reform (*SIW*: 166).

The irresponsibility and insecurity of the Anglo-Irish position is presented in parodic form in *The Last September* through the Montmorencys who have no home of their own but move continually between friends' houses, unhappy, unsettled, and childless, the latter a symbol of Anglo-Irish barrenness, of a race dying out.

Lack of contact with their Irish neighbours exacerbated the siege-like conditions of the Anglo-Irish way of life. In *Bowen's Court*, Bowen contrasts the English squire's readiness to involve himself in the activities of his tenants with the huge walls the Anglo-Irish built around their demesnes cutting themselves off from the language, religion, and national loyalties of the native population, with the result that they lived like 'only children, singular, independent and secretive' (*BC*: 20). In *The Last*

September, Lady Naylor is scornful of her friend Anna Partridge's attempt to involve herself in the lives of her English neighbours. In the absence of political or cultural power, the Anglo-Irish, Bowen argued, put their trust in style and good manners to protect themselves against an inner uncertainty, endeavouring, 'To live as though living gave them no trouble' (*BC*: 456). In her preface to Sheridan Le Fanu's *Uncle Silas*, she explained:

> The hermetic solitude and the autocracy of the great country house, the demonic power of the family myth, fatalism, feudalism and the 'ascendancy' outlook are accepted facts of life for the race of hybrids from which Le Fanu sprang (*MT*: 101).

This heroic myth is carried so far by Lady Naylor that, reversing the British colonial order, she regards the post-war English as markedly inferior to the Anglo-Irish, barely human in fact, restless, vulgar, socialist and disturbingly modern.

Lady Naylor, as meddlesome and class-conscious as Lady Catherine de Bourgh, is one of Bowen's powerful older women who find an outlet for their unused abilities in dominating those around them. In Lady Naylor's case, exercise of power fills a vacuum left by the loss of power and status of the Anglo-Irish male (Lassner, 1990: 33), and the novel submits Anglo-Irish masculinity to a severe critique. Caught between loyalty to his tenants and to the British army, Sir Richard Naylor remains paralysed, plagued with guilt-filled nightmares about the Black and Tans and reluctant to face the knowledge that the English soldier, Gerald Lesworth, a frequent visitor to his house, has most likely been assassinated by his tenants. Hugo Montmorency is well aware that, at a time when masculinity was bound up with a willingness to die in defence of one's country and its women, the political situation in Ireland has robbed Anglo-Irish males of a heroic role. He complains of being 'deprived of heroism by this wet kind of smother of commiseration' (*LS*: 82), which is indeed expressed in the novel by English army wives like Mrs Vermont whose statement, 'We came to take care of all of you' (*LS*: 47), is not well received by the Anglo-Irish. Hugo pushes his emasculation to its logical conclusion by renouncing his ancestral home and adopting what in that period would have been thought of as the female role of caregiver to his wife. Lady Naylor's nephew, Laurence, shares Hugo's feelings of vacancy produced by the political situation: 'I know nothing', he complains, 'this might all just as well be going on in the Balkans' (*LS*: 92). Laurence's desire to make contact with the gunmen is constantly thwarted and when he does finally encounter them, the episode, like much in this novel, is anticlimactic (they simply rob him of his shoes and watch). It is the Anglo-Irish women, Marda and Lois, not Hugo or Laurence, who confront the IRA gunman in the mill.

The generational divide portrayed in *The Hotel*, is particularly acute in the Anglo-Irish context of *The Last September* where the younger generation, represented by Lois and Laurence, both orphans and therefore neither direct heirs to Danielstown, see through the pretense of their elders that everything will carry on as normal. They know their class is about to be superseded and begrudge taking part in a way of life that has no future: 'they both sat eating tea with dissatisfaction, resentful at giving so much of themselves to what was to be forgotten' (*LS*: 118). They chafe against the sacrifice the Big House demands of them, the 'set of coded instructions' as to how they should behave (Kiberd, 1996: 376). They both express a longing for Danielstown to burn: 'I should like to be here when this house burns ... And we shall all be so careful not to notice' (*LS*: 44), Laurence remarks to Hugo, while Lois is prepared casually to sacrifice the family home if its burning down will be a way of impressing them all on Marda's memory. Ian d'Alton has noted the imagery of fire and flames running through *The Last September* that, together with the autumnal colours – orange, red, russet, yellow – prefigure the novel's final scene and the ending, for the Naylors, of the Big House way of life (d'Alton, 2018: 26).

The Last September is centrally a female *Bildungsroman*. Lois recognizes that the particular pattern into which she has been born is in process of disintegrating but, as the new Irish state has yet to come into being, so she has not yet found her path in life. In the opening scene, awaiting the arrival of Hugo and Francie Montmorency, Lois is presented as performing with accuracy the part expected both from Anglo-Irish hospitality and in particular from herself as Sir Richard's niece: 'Lois stood at the top of the steps looking cool and fresh; she knew how fresh she must look, like other young girls' (*LS*: 7). This emphasis on her performance as young woman of the Big House is repeated throughout the novel: 'her youth seemed to her also rather theatrical ... she was only young in that way because people expected it. She had never refused a role' (*LS*: 32).

Lois knows that she and Laurence embody the Big House's hope for the next generation but is puzzled by what awaits her. Laurence has at least Oxford to return to. For Lois, aware that exciting developments are going on around her as the Irish wage their war against the British, her gender is a trap. When Gerald Lesworth, the young English officer who hopes to marry Lois, mentions the recent burning of an army barracks by Irish nationalists, Lois explodes in resentment at the narratives of class and gender that control her life:

> 'Do you know that while that was going on, eight miles off, I was cutting a dress out, a voile that I didn't even need, and playing the gramophone? ... How is it that in this country that ought to be full of such violent realness, there seems nothing for me but clothes and what people say? I might just as well be in some kind of cocoon' (*LS*: 49).

Lois' awareness of the flaws in the role both her gender and her class require her to fulfil leads her to take an interest in the Irish nationalists who haunt the countryside around Danielstown and enter its demesne. Bowen draws a series of intriguing parallels between Lois and the Irish revolutionaries. Both are ignored by the older generation of Anglo-Irish unless circumstances force them on their attention. As her response to the Troubles is to play them down as far as possible, so Lady Naylor is determined not to notice the relationship that has formed between Lois and the unsuitable Gerald until Francie's remarks force her opposition to the match into the open and oblige her to operate guerilla tactics in order to thwart their engagement. When Lois spies a man in a trench-coat hurrying through their demesne, she recognizes that it is pointless to tell the other inhabitants of Danielstown about her exciting encounter since they will not listen. Here Lois' fate and that of the nationalists merge in the Naylors' determination not to know. Conversely, Lois is an irrelevance for the IRA man.

Both Lois and the nationalists are portrayed as rushing to meet their uncertain futures. Marda sums up Lois' eagerness to love using a typical Bowen simile: 'She is in such a hurry, so concentrated upon her hurry, so helpless. She is like someone being driven against time in a taxi to catch a train' (*LS*: 82). Similarly the haste of the man in the trench-coat leads Lois to conclude that 'It must be because of Ireland he was in such a hurry', and she recognises that conceiving of her country emotionally, as he does, is 'something else she could not share' (*LS*: 34). Cut off from the vital Gaelic and Catholic Irish culture, for Lois Ireland is simply 'a way of living, an abstract of several landscapes' (*LS*: 34). This emotional detachment from Irish life goes back to the original sin of colonial misappropriation and the colonists' subsequent refusal to feel guilt or to empathise with the sufferings of their tenants, as Bowen makes clear in *Bowen's Court*: 'The structure of the great Anglo-Irish society was raised over a country in martyrdom. To enjoy prosperity one had to exclude feeling' (*BC*: 248).

As the nationalists have the memory of past rebellions, of 1798 and 1916, to sustain them, so Lois has the memory of her dead mother, Laura, who chafed against the restrictions of Big House living. Laura is remembered as being 'rather a bad hostess' (*LS*: 11), given to 'epic rages', during one of which, 'averting from the stare of the house an angry profile' (*LS*: 107), she fled North to make her ill-fated marriage to Mr Farquar, instead of the more socially acceptable Hugo. For her depiction of Laura, whose inarticulate rage is evident in her sprawling initials and an insulting sketch, probably of Hugo, that Lois finds on the walls of the box room, Bowen draws on Irish Protestant Gothic familiar to her from the work of Sheridan Le Fanu, Charles Maturin and others. Laura haunts Danielstown like a member of the un-dead. Her trunks rotting away in the box room give off an air of oppressive mustiness that seeps through the interior of the Big House, while outside her menacing presence is felt in the damp laurels that clutch at Lois as she hurries through the shrubbery:

> Laurels breathed coldly and close: on her bare arms the tips of leaves were timid and dank, like tongues of dead animals. Her fear of the shrubberies tugged at its chain, fear behind reason, fear before her birth; fear like the earliest germ of her life that stirred in Laura (*LS*: 33).

Her mother's uncanny presence, the sighting of the man in the trench coat, her perception, during an outing with Hugo, of the Anglo-Irish as a transient presence in the Irish landscape, and her shocked realization that she cannot attract Hugo's attention, are all minor disturbances in Lois' outlook; however she has no clear idea of what she would put in place of the Anglo-Irish narrative for her life. An apathy and paralysis that has been likened to the plays of Samuel Beckett keep the young embalmed in the routines of the Big House (Mooney, 2009: 20–1). The vacancy Lois perceives in herself is matched by the vacancy she senses in Danielstown: 'after every return – or awakening, even, from sleep or preoccupation

– she and those home surroundings still further penetrated each other mutually in the discovery of a lack' (*LS*: 166).

Lois knows that she is expected to marry suitably but finds difficulty in setting about this. Her two girlfriends, their names, Viola and Livvy (an abbreviation of Olivia), recalling the leading female characters in *Twelfth Night*, are both more skilled in the world of sexual politics than herself. Viola, the English schoolfriend with whom Lois corresponds, displays in her letters a young woman already accomplished at assessing the suitability of men, provoking in Lois the realization that Viola must have only played at being a schoolgirl as she, Lois, now has to play at being grown up. Lois' Irish friend Livvy, whose enthusiasm for the military rivals that of Lydia Bennet, is similarly effective in stage managing her engagement to the bewildered David. By contrast Lois is uncertain. In Mrs Fogarty's hospitable drawing room, where love songs work on the feelings of the British soldiers and their young women, she protests: 'All that fuss, if you know what I mean, about just somebody' (*LS:* 74).

Engagement to Gerald is Lois' attempt at self-definition: 'it *is* something definite', she thinks (*LS*: 162), a remark she later repeats to Francie. However, as she comes to recognise, marriage to Gerald will be as constraining as life in Danielstown since his sense of chivalry impels him into a protective attitude towards both Lois and Ireland. 'He loved me, he believed in the British Empire' (*LS*: 203), she reflects after his death. For both Lois and Ireland, though, the price of his protection – loss of freedom to act – is too high. She resists Gerald's colonizing efforts and draws a parallel between England's misplaced sense of chivalry in regard to Ireland (their refusal to declare outright war on the country) and male chivalry towards women: 'Can you wonder this country gets irritated? It's as bad for it as being a woman. I never can see why women shouldn't be hit' (*LS*: 49). Lois' moment of outrage only strengthens Gerald's feelings of protectiveness. As a woman she cannot be expected to understand his point of view, just as the

Irish nationalists cannot understand England's. The implication is that Gerald knows what is best for both Lois and Ireland.

Gerald's kiss in the drawing room prompts feelings of loneliness and displacement in Lois, reminding her of the times when she has been seasick, 'locked in misery between Holyhead and Kingstown' (*LS*: 89). Here, Lois' sexual identity and her national identity combine to cause her confusion. As a member of the Anglo-Irish, her identity is forever hyphenated between England and Ireland; as a woman her sexuality remains unaroused by Gerald's kiss. She longs to escape the constraints of both gender – 'I hate women. But I can't think how to begin to be anything else', she tells Marda (*LS*: 99) – and nationality, desiring, in language that reads like proto-Beckett, to be 'enclosed in nonentity, in some ideal no-place' (*LS*: 89). When in her bedroom she overhears Francie and Lady Naylor discussing her, she bangs the water jug down on the basin to get them to stop: 'She didn't want to know what she was, she couldn't bear to: knowledge of this would stop, seal, finish one' (*LS*: 60). The resulting crack in the basin will remain for her as a reminder that her personal, sexual, perhaps even political, identity remains unformed.

The theme of sexual ambiguity reveals another trace of *Twelfth Night* in *The Last September* (Ingman, 2010: 153–65). Patricia Coughlan, who observes that desire possesses 'a strikingly labile quality' in Bowen's work (Coughlan, 1997: 105), reads the electrifying Marda (her name an anagram of drama, as Gerald's surname is an anagram of worthless) as an example of someone who exudes sexual attractiveness for both sexes. Hugo, Laurence and Lois are all attracted to her. The novel opens with Lois' misconceived crush on Hugo, a hangover from childhood. She would love to be able to solve the problem of her future by loving Gerald but, after getting to know Marda, Lois has moments of wanting to be 'a woman's woman' (*LS*: 99) and wishing Gerald 'were a woman' (*LS*: 172). As with Sydney and Mrs Kerr, Lois' attraction to Marda seems more powerful than her feelings for her fiancé: 'Don't you wonder at all if I miss her?' she asks Gerald (*LS*: 153).

In the scene in the abandoned mill (itself a symbol of colonial exploitation), Lois comes up against two realities simultaneously: the reality of Irish hostility towards the Anglo-Irish as the IRA man's gun goes off, and the reality of sexual passion in the violence of Hugo's reaction to Marda's wounding. Having been seduced by Marda into entering the mill, Lois learns that sexual passion is not the respectable indifference she feels for Gerald but something as violent and unpredictable as a gun going off: 'I had no idea – I was too damned innocent', she exclaims (*LS*: 128). The gunman's warning that she may not have Danielstown for much longer, leaves her feeling 'ruled out' from Ireland's future. She realizes that her presence in that country must always have been on sufferance.

For Lois, this is one of those moments when the veneer of civilized life cracks to reveal abysms beneath and Bowen draws an explicit comparison with the fall of the House of Usher in Edgar Allen Poe's novel after a terrible secret has been revealed: 'Cracks ran down; she expected, now with detachment, to see them widen, to see the walls peel back from a cleft – like the House of Usher's' (*LS*: 124). The vocabulary here is saturated with violence and sexuality, and the Gothic overtones in this mill scene, explored by Neil Corcoran, belong to the Protestant Gothic of Anglo-Irish literary imagination which provides space for the fears and suppressed guilt of the colonisers to emerge (Corcoran, 2004: 51–55). The vampiric blood on Marda's lips and the sudden apparition of the pale and hungry IRA man exacting vengeance for past persecutions, point to the return of the undead. Lois makes a pact with Marda not to mention the gunman, as earlier she had kept silent over the intruder on their demesne, thereby sealing her disloyalty to one side of her Anglo-Irish identity and resisting the sacrifice extracted from 'children born within a settler colonial order that prioritized loyalty to an abstract national identity above local cooperation and identification' (Backus, 1999: 19).

There are Gothic overtones too in the scene of the storm-tossed party in the rackety army hut where Lois is disconcerted to find herself intrigued by Gerald's fellow soldier, Daventry. Corcoran notes that Daventry functions as Gerald's satanic other (Corcoran, 2004: 55–60), the two soldiers bound together by the traumas they have undergone in the trenches in the First World War: 'Gerald and Daventry passed in the dark with, it seemed, a queer silent interchange' (*LS*: 153). Daventry, a recognizable 'bounder', is, like Victor Ammering, shell-shocked from the First World War, to such an extent that he seems to Lois to be a ghost, 'not a man … hardly even a person' (*LS*: 157). As in *The Hotel* the First World War, which decimated so many heirs to Irish Big Houses, looms over the post war era. In the photographs of dead soldiers in Mrs Fogarty's drawing-room, in the mention of Marda's first fiancé who died at the Somme, the war is unfinished business that may return to haunt them at any time. Even for Lois, as Bowen is at pains to point out in her preface, 'world war had shadowed her school-days' (*MT*: 126). Her meeting with Daventry is a faint aftershock from the episode in the mill, another of those moments when the veneer of civilized life seems about to crack.

In the end Marda, no help to Lois, capitulates to her society's gender and class expectations by marrying the dull-sounding but respectable Leslie Lawe: 'It's a good thing we can always be women', she remarks (*LS*: 98). Lois' future, like that of Ireland, is left uncertain. After Gerald's death, she is packed off to France to perfect her language, an apparently random choice by her aunt since art school and Italy are what have been talked of most of the novel. None of these options provide a secure future for Lois who knows she does not draw well. In the eyes of her Anglo-Irish family, she has only one destiny – marriage to someone of her own class – but the burning down of Danielstown subsequent to her departure underlines the fact that there can be no return to the fixed patterns of the past for Lois. Whereas Lois' mother lingers in the text like a trapped ghostly presence, haunting Danielstown with her scratching on the walls, her rotting trunks and the memory of her unappeased rages, Lois' future, like Sydney's, is left open.

In *The Last September* Lois awakens to her place in society but also to the fact that she is unable straightforwardly to accept the identity prepared for her by her class and her gender. As an outsider she becomes interested in the nationalists' struggle, an interest she cannot pursue very far because of the constraints of her Anglo-Irishness. Not only do the Naylors discourage her interest in the rebels, but when she does attempt an approach to her Irish neighbours they ignore her (the man in the trench-coat), distrust her (Michael Connor) or threaten her (the IRA man in the mill). The ending may be read as positive – with the burning of Danielstown, Lois escapes anachronistic Anglo-Irish narratives for her life – or, as Derek Hand suggests, in an observation that will resonate through Bowen's later novels: 'Lois' leaving might also signal a future of dislocation from home and family, with her condemned to be a homeless wanderer' (Hand, 2011: 183).

Writing of the Anglo-Irish, Bowen said:

> Ireland had worked on them, through their senses, their nerves, their loves. They had come to share with the people round them sentiments, memories, interests, affinities. The grafting-on had been, at least where *they* were concerned, complete. If Ireland did not accept them, they did not know it – and it is in that unawareness of being looked out at from some secretive, opposed life, that the Anglo-Irish naïve dignity and, even, tragedy seems to me to stand. Themselves, they felt Irish, and acted as Irishmen (*BC*: 160).

In this context, Lois' freedom is not so much a triumphant escape from entrapping narratives as the tragedy of being set adrift in Europe. She confesses to Marda a yearning 'to be in a pattern … to be related' (*LS*: 98), but her home, as the novel makes clear, was always insecure. 'There is no normative, prior place of belonging', Nels Pearson observes in relation to Bowen's protagonists (Pearson, 2015: 75).

Bowen described *The Last September* as of all her books 'the nearest to my heart'. Written in England and at several years remove from the time when, as an adolescent in Bowen's Court, she asked herself '*what* I should be and when?' (*MT*: 123), this female *Bildungsroman* gains in confidence and depth from her first-hand knowledge of the Irish context, resulting in what many readers still regard as her finest novel.

CHAPTER TWO

Interwar Femininity: *Friends and Relations* and *To the North*

Friends and Relations (1931)

In *Friends and Relations*, the crack-up has occurred several decades ago, in the scandalous love affair between Considine Meggatt and Lady Elfrida Tilney, the aftershocks of which reverberate through the novel and threaten to be repeated in the next generation, in the relationship between Janet and her brother-in-law, Edward. Bowen's first novel set in England reveals her feeling her way into her subject. She admitted in an interview broadcast in 1950: 'in some ways that novel was more exterior to me than any other I've ever written before or since' (*LI*: 278). Her relationship with England was always complex and went through several stages. Her statement in *Pictures and Conversations* – 'Possibly, it was England made me as a novelist' (*MT*: 276) – is ambiguous. The context suggests that Bowen meant that England gave her literary networks, publishing opportunities and a chance to realize her ambitions as a writer. However, in light of Bowen's subsequent career, the statement carries an underlying suggestion that as an outsider, particularly an Anglo-Irish outsider who felt that her class had been sold out by the English in 1921, she was better able to look on the assumed moral legitimacy of the English upper middle classes with a satirical eye:

> I arrived, young, into a different mythology – in fact, into one totally alien to that of my forefathers, none of whom had resided anywhere but in Ireland for some centuries ... From now on there was to be (as for any immigrant) a cleft between my heredity and my environment, the former remaining, in my case, the more powerful (*MT*: 276).

Bowen's ignorance of English society prompted her to subject it to scrutiny:

> Submerged, the mythology of this 'other' land could be felt at work in the ways, manners and views of its people, round me; those, because I disliked being at a disadvantage, it became necessary to probe (*MT*: 276).

At times *Friends and Relations* comes close to W. B. Yeats' contempt for the middle classes in its exploration of the moral vacuum at the heart of upper-middle-class English society, Bowen's experience in Ireland as member of a class which spectacularly lost status after the 1921 treaty sensitising her to moments when, as in post-war Britain, a shake up in the class system threatens. And there are faint echoes of Frances Cashel Hoey's novel of romantic entanglements, *All or Nothing* (1888), particularly in the opening scene of a marriage that is fated from the outset, suggesting that Bowen's reading of earlier popular Irish female novelists might bear examination.

Though *Friends and Relations* is often regarded as Bowen's weakest novel, it contains some of her funniest set pieces as well as pursuing her critique of interwar narratives for women's lives. The novel develops, in Anna, Bowen's figure of the perceptive child who, like Cordelia in *The Hotel*, understands too much of the adult world, and portrays, in Theodora, a young woman intent on sabotaging the smooth working of the world of her elders in order to make her mark. Patricia Coughlan has described *Friends and Relations* as expanding '*The Last September*'s enquiry into desire and disruption' (Coughlan, 2018: 214), while Andrew Bennett reads the novel as a study of 'the ethics of a resistance to passion' (Bennett, 2009: 34). Viewed in this light, Bowen's careful exploration of the ethical cost of romantic love and sexual passion in what is a tightly written and tightly plotted novel repays attentive reading.

The year of Laurel Studdart's wedding to Edward Tilney is given simply as 192 – which must be 1920 given that, in the tripartite structure Bowen often favoured for her novels, the second part occurs ten years later, and the final part eleven years after the Tilney marriage, bringing us to 1931, the year of publication. The interwar years in Britain were a period when the narratives for women's lives were particularly restrictive. After their war work in factories, on farms, in hospitals and driving ambulances at the front, employment opportunities dried up and a combination of marriage bars, unequal pay, media images and government campaigns encouraged women back into the home and into their expected roles of wives and mothers (Beddoe, 1989). As the opening of *Friends and Relations* makes clear though, the dearth of young men as a consequence of the war rendered that task more difficult. It is thought in Cheltenham that Mrs Studdart has been remarkably fortunate in marrying off both her daughters, particularly Janet who, in the initial chapters seems set to become that prevalent interwar figure, the daughter at home, the spinster or 'surplus' woman, eking out her time running local societies and directing branches of the Cubs and Girl Guides. As the novel progresses, however, it becomes apparent that the war has had a more profound effect on this society than merely the lack of suitable husbands.

In her essay, 'The Bend Back' (1950), Bowen describes how 'confidence was broken by 1914' (*MT*: 54) and in *The Hotel* and *The Last September*, she portrays young lives continuing to be haunted by the First World War. In *Friends and Relations*, the etiolated lives of the post-war generation are thrown into relief by the insouciance of the older generation. The Studdarts' worries over the close alliance between Tilneys and Meggatts that Janet's marriage to Considine's nephew, Rodney, will bring about are brushed aside by Lady Elfrida with a casualness that shocks them. Not only is she not at all subdued by her status as a *divorcée* in a society where divorce was still rare and largely limited to the upper classes, she even has the effrontery to remain on friendly terms with the co-respondent in her divorce, Considine, who has long since moved on to other lovers. Rejecting the roles of wife and mistress, Lady Elfrida has also thwarted Edward's adolescent desire to play a chivalrous part as his mother's protector. Returning from exile in Paris and, through 'some retreat of prejudice' (*FR*: 68), being accepted back into society, Lady Elfrida leaves Edward, whose views have been formulated for him by a committee of unmarried aunts, 'nonplussed' (*FR*: 24): 'She seemed absolutely contented and talked about Considine as though he were Edward's uncle, till he had to make her see that he couldn't bear it' (*FR*: 25). Like the Anglo-Irish, Lady Elfrida, who may in fact have Irish connections for she is in Ireland at the end of the novel, lives as though living gives her 'no trouble' (*BC*: 456), facing down her contentious past with bravado and concealing her moments of loneliness beneath a stylish social performance.

Careful attention to apparently throwaway lines suggests, however, that, like the Anglo-Irish Naylors, Lady Elfrida is less nonchalant than her social performance suggests. At the Tilney wedding, she is 'for a moment ravaged: she had this less than moment for consternation, her own life was ruined, ruined' (*FR*: 14). She is occasionally plagued by piercingly bleak memories, of the period of public humiliation and loss of self confidence in Paris after her divorce, and of a wretched, solitary Christmas with Edward as a child when she failed to make the day festive for him. Passages such as these, which portray Lady Elfrida as more punished for her behaviour than she cares to admit, suggest that it is possible, as John Coates has argued, to read the novel as condemning the selfishness of adulterous love and affirming the positive value of family life (Coates, 1998: 47–70). However, though the narrator imposes words like 'sin', 'sinner', 'wicked' and 'penitence' on Lady Elfrida and Considine, these labels come to seem like an empty societal reflex holding little meaning for their inner lives. The novel is saturated with a religious vocabulary so conventional and almost infantile that in the end it loses force through repetition, indicating its ineffectiveness as a frame for contemporary living. Though Lady Elfrida has moments of consternation, she accepts love 'as a very high kind of overruling disorder' (*FR*: 104) and mainly regrets her past for the inconvenience it has brought to the younger generation: 'few would for long be easy under a roof with herself. This rueful contemplation of fact, from time to time, was the nearest she ever came to penitence' (*FR*: 39). By the end it is only childlike, undeveloped, characters, Edward and Laurel, or malicious characters like Theodora, who are unable to overlook Lady Elfrida's breach of decorum.

For there is another way of viewing the situation, as Janet points out, in a crucial conversation with her sister. Laurel explains that Edward has been traumatised as a result of being bundled away from his mother as a five-year-old by his aunts:

> 'They came without any explanation and took him away from his home in a cab, so indignantly. He says that's what he remembers so fearfully; nobody would explain. A dreadful house in Buckinghamshire appeared from somewhere and bits of the London furniture kept turning up in it; like wreckage coming down on a flood, he thought' (*FR*: 24).

The echoes here of Bowen's own childhood experience of being sent away from her father's house in Dublin in the middle of the night without explanation and 'taken in a cab to the house of cousins' (Glendinning, 1978: 25) suggest that Bowen was not being entirely open when she described the novel as 'exterior' to herself. The reader's sympathies are not, however, allowed to linger with Edward and his obsessive memories of childhood trauma. Janet, who loves him and deplores 'grievance as a delay of the faculties' (*FR*: 77), points out that Edward could not possibly have thought of all this when he was five and suggests her sister gives him something else to think about. Janet's bracing words imply that an adult world should be able to absorb such traumas. Laurel, whose own arrested girlhood makes her the worst sort of wife for Edward, encourages him to continue to think of himself as a traumatised child and to anchor his identity in his mother's 'infidelity to his childhood' (*FR*: 99) in a way that constantly threatens to fracture the harmonious surface Janet wishes to preserve in her relations with her sister.

In Part Two of the novel, the ancient catastrophe breaks through this civilised veneer when Rodney and Janet, conscious of Considine's boredom, suddenly see no reason why Lady Elfrida, despite Edward's interdiction, should not be allowed to visit Batts at the same time as her former lover. The narrator attempts to draw large moral lessons from their decision:

> Today proved to be one of those weekdays, vacant, utterly without character, when some moral fort of a lifetime is abandoned calmly, almost idly, without the slightest assault from circumstance. So religions are changed, celibacy relinquished, marriages broken up, or there occurs a first large breach with personal honour (*FR*: 69).

The breach of decorum seems, however, eminently practical to Janet since Elfrida and Constantine amuse one another, and she takes the reasonable view that it is good for Edward's children to see their elders happy when once they were so wretched (*FR*: 90). The decision amounts to 'an earthquake' for the emotionally undeveloped Edward and Laurel (*FR*: 70), but in a novel where the wicked (Constantine, Lady Elfrida) more or less flourish while Edward's father 'more notably sinned against' (*FR*: 68) dies of a broken heart, the energy remains with characters like Lady Elfrida as opposed to the pallid, disapproving figures of Edward and Laurel.

The draining of significance from previously vital religious vocabulary is only one aspect of Bowen's presentation of the deterioration of lives in post-war Britain. Lady Elfrida's scandalous prewar abandonment of her marriage and child for a passionate but short-lived affair with Considine haunts and threatens the younger generation, acting both as a warning but also setting a standard by which their passionless marriages are found wanting. Laurel, spurred by 'the catastrophe' (*FR*: 129) into sudden maturity, tells Janet towards the end of the novel: 'this idea of Elfrida, what she had, what she was, has been fearful; it's ruined us all. We've been certain of missing something ...' (*FR*: 129). In comparison with the Edwardian self-confidence of the ex-lovers, the lives of this post-war generation appear enervated. Certainly Considine, veteran of many love affairs, finds the country routine maintained by his nephew and Janet at Batts 'Lenten' (*FR*: 67), a sad come down from the days when he gaily entertained lovers there.

Even the feeling between Janet and Edward is only a faded reflection of Elfrida's passion for Constantine. Believing Janet has gone off with Edward, their friends are shocked at the prospect of a 'catastrophic torrent' (*FR*: 144) wreaking havoc in all their lives, but the lovers do not elope, they remain 'land-bound' (*FR*: 147). When Edward, for whom his mother's behaviour has resulted in 'a dread of love ... a more than moral distaste for the cruel inconvenience, the inconvenient cruelty of passion' (*FR*: 119), confesses to Janet that he has resisted falling in love with her, the phrase 'more than moral distaste' suggests that it is not morality that is impeding the lovers so much as a more fundamental diminishment of feeling. Edward's initial hesitation between the sisters arises, it is suggested, because of his intuition that Janet was more than he could cope with, that she was able to take his measure: 'some glance of hers away from him to perfection of which he could not be aware' (*FR*: 78). '"If you and I had fallen in love – But I didn't want that", he said clearly' (*FR*: 95). Although, under the impulse of passion, Janet experiences moments of fragmenting off into another, darker woman, an uncanny stranger, 'an unborn shameful sister' (*FR*: 122), she is eventually brought to admit that, unlike the Edwardian lovers, she and Edward 'have no – no bitter necessity' (*FR*: 134) to become lovers. Their resistance to adulterous passion may be moral in the conventional sense, preserving marriages, keeping families together, but it is also presented as a flaw, an inability on the part of a generation which has grown up during the war to feel as much as the previous generation: 'their will like a frozen waterfall seemed to be timelessly standing still' (*FR*: 134). In a metaphor borrowed from Katherine Mansfield to suggest their love's barrenness, one of Bowen's many borrowings from Mansfield, the aloe has not flowered (*FR*: 152).

The reverberations of the affair between Considine and Lady Elfrida are felt across more than one generation. Anna Tilney, daughter of Edward and Laurel, is forced by the childishness of both parents to become more mature than her years, while her cousin Hermione, 'a preposterous child for Janet' (*FR*: 56) expresses all the passion her mother has suppressed. Theodora Thirdman, aged fifteen at the time of the Tilney wedding, is able by dint of 'intently listening' (*FR*: 13) to work out the romantic entanglements to which most of her elders remain oblivious. Theodora, prey to jealousy and malice, is one of Bowen's 'young disrupters'. After a childhood abroad, she yearns to make her mark on England and on the adult world, arming herself 'like a bandit, to hold up anything, anyone, and wreak pillage upon the years' (*FR*: 27). Falling in love with Janet, she longs to tear off Janet's mask of composure and get her to admit her feelings for Edward:

> To splinter the vase, to knock the dish out of Janet's hand, Theodora had only to cry: 'You still love him'. A wild enough

kind of justice. But violence was not distasteful to Theodora (*FR*: 78).

Patricia Coughlan astutely links Theodora's desire to disrupt with Lois' wish to see Danielstown burn: 'She triggers the *dénouement* from malice and emotional desperation combined, an intervention structurally paralleling the conflagration desired by Lois' (Coughlan, 2018: 214). Theodora writes the malicious letter that threatens to break apart the world of her elders by confronting Laurel with the truth about Janet's feelings. Yet Theodora, who loves Janet 'beyond propriety' (*FR*: 146), and whose desires thus threaten the prescribed roles for women in this period, is, significantly, the character who escapes the post-war stasis that governs her elders' lives. Her life embraces modernity: as an adolescent she is attached to the telephone, 1930 finds her living with a female friend in a London flat with a modernist décor, pursuing a career, and taking holidays abroad. She has become, as she always wished, an urban sophisticate while retaining sufficient blind passion to cause a fracture in the civilised world of her elders.

Theodora's future is in marked contrast to that of Laurel and Janet. Laurel's sudden awakening to the situation between her husband and her sister makes it seem, in an echo of Lois' shock in the mill, that her house has fallen 'like Usher's cracked through the heart, through the hearth' (*FR*: 145). Yet, despite the chasm that has opened up in their lives, the sisters never succeed in escaping the interwar script for their lives. In the concluding scene, they return virtually to their pre-marital lives, walking into Cheltenham each on their father's arm. As the group pauses outside the hotel Edward stayed in before his wedding, the novel turns back on itself to the moment before the Tilney wedding. Andrew Bennett comments: 'It is a love story … that takes the extraordinary (experimental, even avant-garde) risk of resisting passion and therefore resists narrative movement, development, plot' (Bennett, 2009: 34). Appearances have been preserved at the cost of suppression, glossing over and generally not noticing, but the reader is left to wonder which is worse: a passion that wrecks lives, damages children and marriages and then fizzles out, or a love, like that between Janet and Edward, that never flowers at all?

Is life, as Edward wishes to believe, 'an affair of charm, not an affair of passion' (*FR*: 99)? In a marriage believed now by scholars not to have been fully consummated (Glendinning, 1978: 108; Ellmann, 2004: 32), and at a time when she had yet to embark on her first affair, Bowen may have been working out a theme that had a very personal resonance for her. However, though the civilised surface is preserved in *Friends and Relations*, there are warning signs that the energies that have been suppressed in this first postwar generation may fail to be contained. Future disruption may be in store, from Theodora, from the impassioned Hermione, and in the quietly revolutionary words of Laurel's anguished mother: 'I wish there were something else she could be, not a woman ... *I can't bear life for her!*' (*FR*: 158). Bowen's next novel, *To the North*, all speed and movement in contrast to the stasis of *Friends and Relations*, explores the reverberations from a passion that is not resisted.

To the North (1932)

In contrast to the Edwardian atmospherics of *Friends and Relations*, *To the North* brings us sharply into the modern era. The early years of the twentieth century not only involved the cataclysms of war and revolution, new scientific, philosophical and technological advances, and unprecedented experiments in art and literature, but also the development of modern transport systems (Stevenson, 1990: 25–8), the trains, cars, and planes that play such a crucial role in this novel. The interwar period was an age of speedy communication via the telegram and the telephone, of which Theodora enjoys making malicious use in *Friends and Relations*, and which feature even more centrally in the plotting of *To the North*. Bowen herself thoroughly embraced modernity in the form of the cinema, air travel, modern architecture, and popular journalism and in *Pictures and Conversations* confessed to 'an enthusiastic naivety with regard to transport which …time has not dimmed' (*MT*: 286). She attributed her enthusiasm for travel to having been present as the age of speed 'came into being round me' (*MT*: 287), agreeing with one reader's comment that her characters 'are almost perpetually in transit': 'Zestfully they take ship or board planes: few of them even are *blasés* about railways. Motor-cars magnetize them particularly' (*MT*: 286). The interwar vogue for travel after the restrictions of wartime has been well documented, beginning with Paul Fussell's seminal work, *Abroad: British Literary Travelling Between the Wars* (1980). In Bowen, adapting Walter Pater's well-known sentence at the conclusion of *Renaissance* (1873) about art lending the highest quality to the passing moment, a liking for travel comes to resemble an artist's credo: 'speed is exciting to have grown up with. It alerts vision, making vision retentive with regard to what only may have been seen for a split second' (*MT*: 287).

To the North continues Bowen's previous three novels' examination of the validity of the marriage plot in the lives of the post-war generation and, as in these earlier novels, incorporates references to the wider social and political context here, in 1930s Europe, becoming ever more threatening. An atmosphere of foreboding is built up in the ominous early reference to Cecilia's feeling that she and her fellow travellers on the express train from Milan are in a 'cattle truck' bound for 'execution' (*TN*: 5). Other glancing references to 'strain at home and in Europe' (*TN*: 177), to this 'uneasy century' (*TN*: 63), and to a cat called Benito, underline the external sense of menace. Even before the tragic conclusion, *To the North* is, as Andrew Bennett and Nicholas Royle observe, 'shadowy with death' (Bennett and Royle, 1995: 35). Though focusing to a large extent on the inner lives of her characters, Bowen employs a combination of realism and modernism in order to incorporate such explicit historical signposts. In this, Chris Hopkins has argued, she seems to be testing the two types of writing against each other, Evelyn Waugh's external satire on restless moderns in *Vile Bodies* (1930) against Virginia Woolf's exploration of her characters' interiority (Hopkins, 2006: 32). The combination of the two modes suggests that Bowen saw neither as entirely adequate by themselves, realism lacking the possibility of expressing the inner consciousness of her characters, the subjective missing the wider social and cultural context. No less than *The Last September*, *To the North* is 'fiction with the texture of history', and Diana Hirst has explored the way in which Bowen, who originally trained as an artist, employs techniques from Futurism and Vorticism to portray the economic, political and social fragmentations of the early 1930s (Hirst, 2018: 63–74).

Much of the contemporary social context in *To the North* is expressed through exploring the impact of modern technology on people's lives, technology often seeming to control humans rather than the other way round. The lurching of the express train from Italy, 'lashing about its passengers as though they were bound to a dragon's tail' (*TN*: 9), precipitates Cecilia's first meeting with Markie that sets the plot in motion, though not in the way a reader of romances might expect. Anthropomorphic machines set the scene for high drama in Lady Waters' home: 'her smallest clock struck portentously, her telephone trilled from the heart, her dinner-gong boomed a warning' (*TN*: 12). The overcautious Julian is nudged into proposing to Cecilia by 'the speed of the car through the glowing country' (*TN*: 109). As well as precipitating action, technology has an emotional effect on these characters. Telephones unanswered make Gerda feel 'quite in disgrace' (*TN*: 90), whereas Cecilia, full of nervous fatigue, senses that she does not exist without her phone: 'Cecilia felt herself crystallize over the wire' (*TN*: 29). Untelephoned, 'she ran down like a clock whose hands falter and point for too long at one hour and minute' (*TN*: 134). Decades before the age of smart phones and social media,

Cecilia is an example of technology overloading the human nervous system.

Marinetti's Futurist manifesto placed the motor car at the heart of its declaration of a new world and Wendy Gan notes: 'The car as represented in early twentieth-century texts has always signified a particular kind of kinetic and aggressive modernity, mostly because of its capacity for speed and fragmentation' (Gan, 2009: 64). During the last disastrous car ride of Emmeline and Markie northwards out of London, it is the car that seems to be in control: 'the little car, strung on speed, held unswerving way' (*TN*: 245). Speed disassembles Emmeline's already fragile identity in a way that recalls a passage in Virginia Woolf's *Orlando* (1928):

> The process of motoring fast out of London so much resembles the chopping up small of identity which precedes unconsciousness and perhaps death itself that it is an open question in what sense Orlando can be said to have existed at the present moment (Woolf, 2000: 200–1).

Orlando is saved, as Emmeline is not, by entering the countryside, allowing her a moment of solitude and reflection in which partly to reassemble her identity.

People become dehumanised by their machines. Miss Tripp (her name cleverly evoking both a short circuit and the travel agency in which she works), is referred to by both Emmeline and Peter as 'the stenographer' and unsurprisingly feels treated like 'an automaton' in the office (*TN*: 122) until one afternoon her emotions get the better of her and she has to be replaced by Miss Armitage who, all briskness and efficiency, really is an automaton, clicking reproach at her employers 'like a waiting taxi' (*TN*: 190). Markie, rising barrister and restless young man unscrupulous in his dealings with young women – 'a bore, a bounder, an egotist, altogether a frightful young man', Cecilia decides (*TN*: 96) – is adept at conversation in a competitive social setting but unresponsive at home. For Markie, technology becomes a convenient means of avoiding unwanted human intimacy: he lives alone in a flat at the top of his sister's house and orders his meals through a speaking-tube.

The characters in *To the North* may not be Anglo-Irish but they are similarly conscious of a vacuum in their lives and at least one critic has drawn a connection between modernist dislocation and Bowen's Anglo-Irish sensibility (Kreilkamp, 2009: 13). The Roman colonists, whose ruined villa Lady Waters and her party visit may, like the Anglo-Irish, have felt themselves exiles in their own homes, but modern life produces its own variations on estrangement: 'Here, where exiles had lived, today's little party of exiles cast round in spirit, to find nothing …' (*TN*: 63). Cecilia, originally married to Emmeline's brother, Henry, is a widow, like so many women in the aftermath of the First World War, though Henry has died, unheroically, of pneumonia. The cataclysm in these two women's lives has already occurred before the opening of the novel: 'their eyes met across a grave' (*TN*: 13). In a lengthy evocative passage at the end of Chapter Twelve, the trauma of Henry's death for Cecilia is likened to the fall of an Anglo-Irish Big House: like 'a great house' 'destroyed by fire – left with walls bleached and ghastly and windows gaping with the cold sky – the master has not, perhaps, the heart or the money to rebuild' (*TN*: 99). Her life now resembles the inferior villas that grow up where the Big House once was, lively with 'brave' little shops and 'radiant picture palaces' (*TN*: 99). 'Life here is livable, kindly and sometimes gay' but 'the great house with its dominance and its radiation of avenues is forgotten' (*TN*: 100). Hollowed out by Henry's death, Cecilia is unable to love wholeheartedly again: 'brave when her house fell, she could not regain some entirety of the spirit. Disability seems a hard reward for courage' (*TN*: 100).

Although Cecilia and Emmeline have managed to paper over the cataclysm by sharing a house in St John's Wood, the permanence of their home is always under threat as first Julian and then

Markie, brought in by Cecilia to the house in Oudenarde Road, precipitate crises. Despite interwar propaganda around women and the home, home is an illusory safe space in *To the North*: 'Houses shared with women are built on sand', Emmeline reflects (*TN*: 208). In widowhood Cecilia has sustained bravado for a while but eventually falls back on engagement to the cautious, uncertain Julian, betraying her home with Emmeline and 'the unspoken good faith' of their 'quiet marriage' (*TN*: 148), for a man for whom she feels at best lukewarm. Emmeline envisages the end of their home together as another conflagration: 'Timber by timber, Oudenarde Road fell to bits, as small houses are broken up daily to widen the roar of London. She saw the door open on emptiness: blanched walls as though after a fire' (*TN*: 207–8).

Julian, like Cecilia, is aware of a vacuum inside himself, worrying that nothing in him can respond naturally to his orphaned niece Pauline's 'diligently little-girlish' performance (*TN*: 36). In common with all Bowen's orphans, fourteen-year-old Pauline yearns for attention and acceptance from the adult world: 'Like a bear you have to keep on throwing buns at', Julian complains (*TN*: 37). Sharing the post-war enervation of the lovers in *Friends and Relations*, he wonders whether Cecilia is worth the effort he has to put into their relationship and finds himself vaguely attracted to Emmeline. When he observes that they live in a restless age, Lady Waters suggests that this restlessness is not simply physical but emotional: '"All ages are restless ... but *this* age", Lady Waters went on, "is far more than restless: it is decentralized. From week to week, there is no knowing where anyone is"', before adding, significantly, '"Myself, I move very little"' (*TN*: 170). Lady Waters' Edwardian standards and expectations are no longer relevant for the younger generation, however, and cause actual harm in relation to Emmeline.

The novel may end with an engagement between Cecilia and Julian but nothing about these two dilatory and inadequate lovers suggests that this is a conventional happy ending. The romance narrative is further put under pressure by Bowen's portrait of the emotional chaos of their contemporaries, none of whose lives – the Blighs' unsteady marriage, Tim Farquarson's broken engagement, Marceline's unhappy lesbianism, Miss Tripp's excessive emotional attachment to Emmeline – fit the traditional marriage plot. Lady Waters' half-baked reading of Freud and Adler leads her to exaggerate the erotic confusions of the young people around her, making her 'quick to detect situations that did not exist' (*TN*: 12) and resulting in much bungled meddling on her part. The first English translation of Freud's work was published in 1909. It was quickly followed by popular books explaining his ideas to the general public so that by the time of Bowen's novel some of the more obvious theories connected with his name (repression, sublimation, dreams, the Oedipus complex) would have been known at second hand to the general public and were regularly referenced in both literary and middlebrow fiction (Beauman, 1983: 147–172). In *To the North*, Freud and his disciples have rendered this interwar generation alarmingly self-conscious and over-analytical about love so that marital happiness seems unachievable. Gerda, 'having read a good many novels about marriage, not to speak of some scientific books … now knew not only why she was unhappy but exactly how unhappy she could still be' (*TN*: 52).

Wendy Parkins has suggested that '*To the North* does not uncritically embrace modernity and its liberatory potential for women' (Parkins, 2001: 84). This sense that the modern age may bring uneven benefits for women is particularly apparent in the fate of Emmeline, 'step-child of her uneasy century' (*TN*: 63), who enjoys nothing more than to take afternoon tea with Sir Robert and the vicar at Farraways, when the house is disembarrassed of the very contemporary presences of Lady Waters' unhappy young guests. Yet Emmeline is also an up-to-date urban professional woman, co-owner of a successful travel agency in Bloomsbury, living an independent life with her sister-in-law and driving herself to parties in her own car. For Bowen to describe a professional woman is rare and, though she always denied she was a feminist, the dialogue in which the controlling Markie suggests Emmeline give up her job because it impinges on their time together is pointedly satirical:

> 'But I don't want to. What should I do all day?'
> 'I don't know: why do anything special?'
> 'I don't know: why do you?' (*TN*: 177).

Markie, the ambitious barrister, naturally ignores 'this silly question' (*TN*: 177).

Despite the feminist undertones of this dialogue, appearances are deceptive for Emmeline strikes others as distant, almost ethereal, the noun 'angel' being often ascribed to her, not because of her goodness, but because her gaze so frequently seems to be focused elsewhere. Her myopic, unearthly presence is associated with transparent or reflective surfaces such as mirrors, ice, silver, crystal, glass, windows, water, in an elaborate pattern of imagery that both suggests blank, reflective innocence and prophesies tragedy. Until she meets Markie, no one has properly registered with Emmeline. Her detachment from ordinary human interchange is summed up in an eerie phrase that has its origins in *Mark* 8: 24, 'she saw men as trees walking' (*TN*: 26), and echoes Bowen's description of her own father's abstractions (Glendinning, 1978: 11).

The instabilities of modern experience are played out in Emmeline's conflicting desires for speed and rootedness. She may drive a car and own a travel agency with the slogan 'Move dangerously', but what Emmeline most yearns for is to be located:

> She longed suddenly to be fixed, to enjoy an apparent stillness, to watch even an hour complete round one object its little changes of light, to see out the little and greater cycles of day and season in one place, beloved, familiar, to watch shadows

move round one garden, to know the same trees in spring and autumn and in their winter forms (*TN*: 144).

In *Pictures and Conversations*, Bowen points out that in a speed-obsessed culture the yearning for stillness may be accentuated: 'Permanence, where it occurs, and it does occur, stands out the more strongly in an otherwise ephemeral world. Permanence is the attribute of recalled places' (*MT*: 287).

The contradictions of modernity are evident in Emmeline's life: she lives a modern urban life but yearns for a home in the country, as revealed poignantly in the scene in Connie Pleach's cottage when she attempts, clumsily, to enact a domesticity Markie does not desire. If her affair with Markie shows Emmeline in one sense to be a modern woman, willing to sleep with him after he has ruled marriage out of the question, it also reveals her as tragically unable to take a light, modern view of passion. In this love affair (her first) with the worldly and practised Markie, 'perplexed by some new view of life that, not quite her own, lent double strangeness to everything' (*TN*: 140), Emmeline entirely loses her bearings. She becomes as dislocated in love as 'a gentle foreigner at Victoria, not knowing where to offer her ticket, to whom if, at all, her passport, uncertain even whether she has arrived' (*TN*: 70). There are no passports for people like us, she tells Markie, whereas 'people married, have passports everywhere' (*TN*: 211).

Emmeline knows that her feelings about Markie can never be revealed to Cecilia who since Henry's death has depended on Emmeline's tranquillity: 'Henry's death had been something ravaging, disproportionate; around Oudenarde Road a kind of pale was put up against one kind of emotion: nothing on that scale was to occur again' (*TN*: 148). She understands that Cecilia would think Emmeline 'ruined' and blame herself (*TN*: 211). Emmeline's betrayal of their home precedes Cecilia's, though remains concealed from her. Echoing Anglo-Irish insecurity after 1921, 'Emmeline, looking across the Channel, suddenly felt a stranger in her own home, a home she had perhaps never fully inhabited' (*TN*: 148). Her love affair has put her, in the Irish phrase, 'beyond the Pale'.

Disorientated by her love affair with Markie, Emmeline finds language inadequate to express her feelings: 'We should be dumb', she thinks, 'there should be other means of communication' (*TN*: 71). 'Perhaps some day words will be different or there will be others' (*TN*: 102), she reflects. As Trinh T. Minh-ha has observed:

> The voyage out of the (known) self and back into the (unknown) self sometimes takes the wanderer far away to a motley place where everything safe and sound seems to waver while the essence of language is placed in doubt and profoundly destabilised. Travelling can thus turn out to be a process whereby the self loses its fixed boundaries (Minh-ha, 1994: 23).

This loss of 'fixed boundaries' is what happens to Emmeline who, in their love affair, travels further in passion than Markie, a shallow sensualist, wishes to go. He feels 'overshot', 'outdistanced' (*TN*: 142), puzzled as to why she does not display the repentance and guilt of a more conventional woman. Such lordly ignoring of the conventions alarms him, 'making him feel, perhaps for the first time, not quite all he could wish' (*TN*: 70). A sexual opportunist who takes his love affairs lightly Markie, reading aloud a lengthy passage from *De L'Amour* in which Stendhal delicately analyses the different stages a lover undergoes, declares: 'One's got no time for all that' (*TN*: 204). He rails against Emmeline's 'too high idea of life' (*TN*: 183), insisting that 'one can't live on the top of the Alps' (*TN*: 183).

At the same time Markie is uneasily aware that his relationship with Emmeline is revealing inadequacies that he has carefully organised his life to conceal: he does not drive and is a nervous flyer, whereas Emmeline is prepared to take risks both in cars and in love. Toppling tower imagery expresses both Emmeline's reckless passion and Markie's fear:

> The tall tower, that rocked by some shock at its base or some flaw in its structure totters and snaps in the air, falls wide; the damage is far-flung: you cannot stand back enough, it is upon you. Markie, in whom something cowered, was much afraid for himself (*TN*: 184).

Preferring to be the one in control, he reverts to the undemanding Daisy on whom he can work off his Byronic complex. Markie, who likes his women 'affable' (*TN*: 9) and 'lowish' (*TN*: 179), finds himself brought up short by Emmeline, a woman outside his range of experience. His rational approach to life is revealed to be insufficient as Gothic melodrama, a touch of Anglo-Irish literary tradition prepared for in the recurring symbolism of burning houses, erupts into his very twentieth-century life in the form of Emmeline's final, insane death drive.

Markie's failure to provide Emmeline with a home, or even any moments of peace and security, is compounded by the predicted loss of the St John's Wood house and the death of the Farraways vicar, marking the end of yet another of her safe places. For the rationalist Markie religion is 'an oppressive monument to futility' (*TN*: 151), but Emmeline makes friends with the vicar and willingly accompanies Sir Robert to church. In *A Time in Rome*, Bowen observes of the ancient Romans: 'Were they not better for two things, devotion to ceremonial, faith in tradition? Once one breaks with either, endless unease begins' (*TR*: 103). Markie's rejection of Christianity leaves his mind

> restless with superstition: like natives before the solid advance of imperial forces, aspiration, feeling, all sense of the immaterial had retreated in him before reason to some craggy hinterland where, having made no terms with the

conqueror, they were submitted to no control and remained a menace (*TN*: 150).

Forced to keep these 'savages' at bay, Markie resorts to what the narrator describes as a 'smallish, over-clear view of life' (*TN*: 151), consonant with Bowen's view of atheism as claustrophobic (Laurence, 2019: 253). The willingness of the church-going Emmeline to sleep with him – 'the complete moral calm with which she had stepped in Paris over one line in behaviour' (*TN*: 182) – surprises and shocks Markie but her attitude reflects that of Bowen herself. According to her first biographer, Bowen 'assumed in Him an understanding of, if not a disregard for, the discreet breaking of society's rules, including its sexual rules, even when these are given the sanction of religion' (Glendinning, 1978: 295–6).

Her love for Markie drives Emmeline to the point of insanity, her single-minded passion destroying any happiness in her daily life, her home or her work, which goes to pieces:

> She bought note-paper from the cashier and wrote, for the first time, to Markie. He did not answer. That week, her hair went dark and dull, her face white: if anyone looked at her in the streets it was to wonder from what she was running away. Broken up like a puzzle the glittering summer lay scattered over her mind, cut into shapes of pain that had no other character. Walking the streets blindly she did not know what she thought, till a knuckle grazed on a wall, a shout as she stepped off into the traffic recalled her from depths whose darkness she had not measured (*TN*: 225).

Such passages make clear Emmeline's shattered state of mind and it is worth remembering that Bowen's father, whose name, Henry, is given to Cecilia's dead husband, was also prone, as Bowens tended to be, to manic obsessions (Laurence, 2019: 16–27). Henry

Bowen died in 1930 after a recurrence of insanity witnessed by his daughter who helped nurse him at the end. Mental illness would therefore have been in Bowen's thoughts at this period.

Total breakdown is as far as cataclysm can go in private life and this time the disaster is not covered over. *To the North* is characteristic of Bowen's novels to date in referencing its beginning in its end: in *The Hotel* there is the quarrel then reconciliation between Miss Pym and Miss Fitzgerald, in *The Last September* Danielstown welcomes visitors in the opening scene and watches the departure of a different kind of visitor at the end, while *Friends and Relations* is bracketed by opening and closing references to the Tilney wedding. Similarly, *To the North* begins and ends with menacing journeys to the north, yet the novel retains an open-endedness that defies its apparent resolution. The onward movement of time is suspended as Cecilia is left with Julian, engaged but as yet unmarried, in the house in Oudenarde Road that she has already in her imagination quitted, endlessly waiting for Emmeline to return home.

CHAPTER THREE

Widening the Scene: *The House in Paris* and *The Death of the Heart*

The House in Paris (1935)

The House in Paris inaugurates a run of three novels that brought Bowen popular and critical success partly because, however obliquely, they capture the *zeitgeist* of the period leading up to and during the Second World War. Set in France, England and Ireland, portraying the darkening European scene and alluding to English and French antisemitism of the 1930s, *The House in Paris* confirms Bowen as a cosmopolitan writer. In *To the North*, France plays a role through the referencing of such authors as Stendhal and Flaubert, and Paris is the place where Emmeline's affair is first consummated, while *The House in Paris*, with its elegant structure and psychological intensity, has been compared to a French novel (Corcoran, 2004: 88–9). Tightly patterned both in imagery and plot, *The House in Paris* adopts Bowen's favourite, tripartite structure, the first and third sections taking place in the present, while the middle section goes back into the past to reveal the initial cataclysm the ramifications of which, though concealed for a long time, affect the lives of all the characters in the present.

Bowen first visited France in 1920 and by the early 1930s she was immersed in French literature (*MT*: 198). Her male lovers in these 1930s novels – Markie, Max, Eddie – all bear faint traces of the nakedly ambitious Julien Sorel of Stendhal's *Le Rouge et le noir* (1830) and it was from the French novel, together with the Russian, that Bowen learned the importance of setting personal life in a wider social and political context, something she claimed very few English novelists, apart from Fielding and Thackeray, managed to do (*MT*: 159).

'Ireland in some ways resembles France' (*CS*: 780), reflects the narrator of Bowen's short story, 'A Day in the Dark' (1956), and in her essay, 'The Idea of France', Bowen expands on the tie between the two countries: 'Traditionally, of course, the idea of France has always had a strong hold over Irish people. France was the friend of hope, of those who for centuries had struggled for Irish freedom' (*PPT*: 62). French aid for Irish revolutionaries did not, as she makes clear, play any part in her own Protestant, Unionist family's liking for France. The Anglo-Irish, French-speaking ladies of her mother's generation looked to France for culture, style, and etiquette, the qualities that mothers hope will be instilled in their daughters when they send them to Mme Fisher's guesthouse in Paris. Bowen does though concede that this Anglo-Irish generation's cult of all things French was partly motivated by 'subtle and un-political anti-Englishness – for in fact they did not always admire the England that they did not fail to support' (*PPT*: 63). Bowen's positioning of France and Ireland as allies against England is reflected in *The House in Paris*, which draws together these two countries through the maturing process Karen Michaelis undergoes in both, in contrast to the ossified English household in which she has grown up.

As in *To the North*, travel plays an important part in *The House in Paris* which opens with two displaced children, refugees almost, stranded for the day in Mme Fisher's house in Paris. One is the motherless English child, eleven-year-old Henrietta, sent by her widowed father to stay with her grandmother in Mentone. For Henrietta, Paris is linked with violence and revolution, the early morning barred windows with strong grilles looking 'ready for an immediate attack (Henrietta had heard how much blood had been shed in Paris)' (*HP*: 22). The other child in Mme Fisher's house is nine-year-old Leopold, of Jewish, French, and English extraction, summoned from Spezia to meet his unknown English mother about whom he has long fantasised and whom he hopes will rescue him from his despised foster parents, the American Grant Moodys.

Subsequent events in the house create an uneasy alliance between the two children against the needless obscurities of an adult world, for the more she learns about Leopold's circumstances, the more Henrietta feels she has dropped down a well 'into something worse than the past in not being yet over' (*HP*: 50). Her prim, Alice in Wonderland English persona, constructed around a series of prejudices, is disturbed by this day of Leopold's crisis in ways that will likely have long term repercussions on her life: 'Today was to do much to disintegrate Henrietta's character' (*HP*: 25). Part One ends with Mme Fisher's daughter, Naomi, reading Leopold a telegram to say that after all his mother Karen cannot come today. Part Two turns back to the past to give an explanation, without grown-up obfuscations and falsifications, of the circumstances of Leopold's birth that have led to his mother being afraid to meet him. It is an account of such directness that would not have been possible for the adult Karen addressing the child Leopold in real life, but is possible in the potential realms of heaven or art, 'with truth and imagination forming every word' (*HP*: 67).

The House in Paris is centred around three contrasting households: Mme Fisher's claustrophobic Gothic house in Paris, aunt Violet's death-shadowed villa in County Cork, and the Michaelis' light, airy upper-middle-class home in London's Regent's Park. The Michaelis home embodies the stability, serenity, and decorum of the English liberal tradition, pre-war values perhaps, but not yet, in the early 1930s, quite out of date. The daughter of the house, Karen, understands that her 'inherited world' might not last and for that reason, though she sometimes wishes to escape it, stands 'obstinately' by it (*HP*: 71). Ray Forrestier fits into this world; indeed, he and Karen are distant cousins. When, her art career faltering, Karen agrees to marry Ray, she knows that in doing so she is falling back 'on her mother's view of things' (*HP*: 69).

Like Bowen's earlier female protagonists (Sydney, Lois, Cecilia), Karen believes her engagement will locate her and provide her with a sense of purpose. At the same time, though she is now on solid ground, she is conscious of her world narrowing. In such moods, like earlier Bowen heroines, she yearns for revolution: 'With Ray I shall be so safe. I wish the Revolution would come soon; I should like to start fresh while I am still young, with everything that I had to depend on gone' (*HP*: 86). She recognises that in her parents' eyes change can only mean loss: at the apex of society, the Michaelis family, like the Anglo-Irish Naylors, has nowhere to go but down. Change is already evident, however, in the erosion of male authority following the First World War. Mr Michaelis, one of Bowen's post-war ineffective male characters, is sidelined as an authority in the home, as the Anglo-Irish male, Sir Richard, was marginalised in Danielstown. Like the Anglo-Irish Naylors, the English Michaelis family express loyalty to a way of life that, in this post-war era, is becoming untenable.

That the Michaelis' values of liberalism, tolerance and niceness will be insufficient to withstand the rise of fascism across Europe becomes apparent when Karen's passion for Max Ebhart, a Jew of mixed French and English ancestry, threatens to disrupt the entire household and its way of life. Mrs Michaelis moves swiftly to contain the catastrophe, fighting to preserve her home and its values by adopting a policy of silence in the face of rebellion that recalls the Anglo-Irish Naylors' strategy of turning a blind eye to the Irish struggle for independence going on around them:

> Karen saw what was ruthless inside her mother. Unconscious things – the doors, the curtains, guests, Mr Michaelis – lent themselves to this savage battle for peace. Sun on the hall floor, steps upstairs in the house had this same deadly intention not to know (*HP*: 173).

In an effort to wrest power from her mother and affirm to herself the reality and importance of her night with Max, Karen breaks the silence between them. Mrs Michaelis counters by downplaying the importance of the affair, painting Max as a Jew on the make: 'no Jew is unastute' (*HP*: 176). In the casual antisemitism of Mrs Michaelis' words, the supposed liberalism of upper-middle-class Englishness is revealed to be nothing more than 'worldliness beginning so deep down that it seems to be the heart' (*HP*: 174).

Max, an outsider in France where he is trying to establish himself in the banking world but where, as Mme Fisher warns him, he will always have to work harder than anyone else to be accepted, is also an outsider in the upper-middle-class English world of the Michaelis family. In loving him, Karen finds herself in a foreign country. Their affair takes place on the margins of England and France (Hythe, Boulogne) indicating the unacceptability of their relationship which, as Karen realises, can only function outside established domestic spaces:

> Karen, walking by Max, felt more isolated with him, more cut off from her own country than if they had been in Peru. You feel most foreign when you no longer belong where you did (*HP*: 157).

In such passages *The House in Paris* refers, albeit obliquely, to the cultural and political instability of 1930s Europe and to a civilisation in crisis. As Phyllis Lassner and Paula Derdiger have observed:

> Regardless of how insular or stable, domestic space in Bowen's writing is never merely private, but rather always generative of and invaded by the history and politics constituting the public sphere (McGarrity and Culleton, 2009: 195).

It is possible to interpret this concern with the wider political context as an Anglo-Irish trace in Bowen's work: having lived through, albeit somewhat remotely, a revolution in her country, she was acutely aware of how private lives can be threatened by public crisis. Mrs Michaelis' private antisemitism had a public parallel in the rise of Oswald Mosley's British Union of Fascists which in 1934 held the infamous Olympia rally in London. In a wider context, Jean Radford notes that under the Nuremberg Laws introduced by the Nazi government in Germany in 1935, even part Jews like Max and his son, Leopold, would be categorised as Jews and deprived of German citizenship (Radford, 1999: 33–45). In France too there was a rise in nationalism and xenophobia against immigrants in the 1930s: Max's feeling that he lacks a home, corroborated by Karen's sense of being an outsider when she is with him, is not merely subjective but a product of the worsening political situation across Europe.

In one way Mrs Michaelis triumphs for she dies knowing that, with Leopold's birth concealed, appearances have been preserved and her daughter's social position secured, but it is a victory won at the price of her life. The description of her dying 'more or less peacefully' (*HP*: 219) shortly after Karen's marriage to Ray sounds terribly ironic and reflects the self-harming silence of the British Establishment around events in Germany prior to the Second World War. Since Mme Fisher's house in Paris is where Karen first meets Max, Lassner and Derdiger read the Michaelis' London home as 'ultimately destabilized by the violent Gothic shadows cast by the house in Paris, a sign of the new global political primitivism – fascism' (McGarrity and Culleton, 2009: 203).

However, in *The House in Paris*, there are not just the two opposing households, French and English, there is also aunt Violet's villa in Rushbrook, County Cork. The Part One scenes in Mme Fisher's house in Paris are immediately followed in Part Two by a flashback to Karen's boat trip to visit her aunt in Ireland, thereby linking the two countries. Karen, chafing against the easy conformism of her engagement to Ray and her family's oppressive congratulations, seeks escape from her too solid English home with her mother's sister in Ireland, a country which, though now at peace, still seems to aunt Violet's relatives insecure compared with England, 'as though she had chosen to settle on a raft' (*HP*: 76).

At first sight, Ireland where revolution has successfully taken place, appears to Karen to prove that transformation is not always the disaster her family fears. Even though her uncle's Big House, Montebello, was burned down in the Troubles, the new state has compensated him for his loss, allowing him to build a new home, Mount Iris, overlooking Cobh, formerly Queenstown, a place 'full of Protestant gentry, living down misfortunes they once had' (*HP*: 75). Even after revolution, things can be smoothed over, Karen realises: 'none of them, as a matter of fact, had done too badly' (*HP*: 75). Appearances are deceptive however: this 'nineteenth-century calm' marks off Rushbrook from the rest of 1930s Ireland struggling to establish its vision for an economically self-sufficient republic distinguished from its larger neighbour by the purity of its values and religion, 'a frantic or lonely dream', as the narrator describes it (*HP*: 75). For Karen, Ireland retains 'a troubling strangeness' (*HP*: 76), a feeling that is vindicated when she discovers that Mount Iris' tranquillity is only apparent, its serene surface willed by her aunt to cover up the fact of her dying.

Ireland plays a pivotal part in the novel for it is where Karen, unsettled by her aunt's questions, starts to rethink her future: 'something in Ireland bends one back on oneself', she tells Ray (*HP*: 89). Her aunt's gentle probing provides Karen with another point of view from that prevailing in her English home with the result that Cork, as much as Paris, is responsible for the cataclysm following Karen's rebellion against her safe engagement with Ray. Her aunt Violet's death is the first frightening 'crack across the crust of life' for the Michaelis household (*HP*: 127), robbing Mrs Michaelis of confidence and clarifying Karen's feelings for Max, bearing out Nels Pearson's observation that in this novel the world view of upper-middle-class English liberal complacency is 'cracked open by Jewish and Irish counternarratives' (Pearson, 2015: 97).

If life in the Michaelis household is carefully edited to present a rational, civilised surface, the atmosphere in Mme Fisher's cramped, claustrophobic house in Paris, where Karen first meets Max, is full of suppressed rage. In its Gothic touches – the red wallpaper striped like bars in the hallway, the airless sick room, 'the charnel convent parlour' (*HP*: 215), Mme Fisher as a witch or vampire preying on the young – several critics have discerned parallels with Sheridan Le Fanu's Gothic novel, *Uncle Silas* (Lee, 1999: 80; Johnson, 2011: 216).

A governess in England before her marriage Mme Fisher, with the help of her daughter, Naomi, has been obliged by widowhood to open a guest house in Paris for English and American young women taking courses in art or music before their inevitable marriages. Mme Fisher has played the role of surrogate mother to the 'daughters' in her charge. Her controlling tactics, reminiscent of Mme Beck's surveillance of adolescent girls in Charlotte Brontë's *Villette* (Lee, 1999: 81), are all the more terrifying for being invisible:

> She asked no questions, but knew: she knew where you went, why, with whom and whether it happened twice. Though Paris was large, you were never out of her ken (*HP*: 103).

A malevolent version of those intrusive older women in Bowen's earlier fiction – Lady Naylor, Lady Waters – Mme Fisher is, in Phyllis Lassner's words, 'a woman who uses motherhood for power she cannot find anywhere else' (Lassner, 1990: 83).

With young women shortly to be absorbed into marriage Mme Fisher's power is necessarily limited and it is in her relationship with Max Ebhart, the Jewish outsider struggling to make his mark in Paris, that she discerns a greater opportunity for influence. Mme

Fisher wishes to mould Max, a rootless Jew, in order to give him access to the power she herself has been denied in a masculinist society and for a time she is successful: 'As she saw me, I became', Max tells Karen (*HP*: 138). Ambivalently in love with him, Mme Fisher controls not only Max's career but also his sexuality. She opposes Max's engagement to her daughter, encouraging him to set his sights higher and is delighted to hear he has 'secured' his position with Karen but then destroys his belief in this love by casting doubts on his motives. When he realises that by marrying Karen he will not be exercising free will but falling in with Mme Fisher's manipulations for his future, Max takes his own life. Mme Fisher becomes for Max the engulfing mother, swallowing up his attempts at independence by her terrible understanding of him. 'My mother was at the root of him', Naomi tells Karen (*HP*: 182) but, in a patriarchal society, the exercise of power is deadly for the mother figure. After Max's death, Mme Fisher's aggression turns inward and she lies on her sickbed in 'passionate un-resignation' (*HP*: 47), the image of frustrated power. In her close reading of this passage in *Pictures and Conversations*, Bowen categorises it as 'an evocation of action thwarted (or withheld energy)' (*MT*: 284).

Both Naomi and Karen are daughters damaged by the intergenerational struggle with their mothers. Masochistic and self-sacrificing Naomi, of mixed English and French parentage and therefore, like Max, unrooted, is the characteristically ineffective daughter of a tyrannising mother. Trained to aid her mother in turning out socialised young girls, she seems the epitome of calm but, as Karen recognises, she is not Mme Fisher's daughter for nothing: 'Under her unassumingness, Naomi had a will that, like a powerful engine started up suddenly, made everything swerve' (*HP*: 101). She forces Karen and Max to meet to test their feelings for each other, a meeting that drastically alters the course of all their lives. Later she takes control of Leopold's destiny by placing him with the Grant Moodys, a placement that turns out to be a disaster. Naomi is constantly smoothing things over in the Paris house, but children, her scattered knitting needles, her own mother, all threaten the 'pretence of safety' (*HP*: 52) that she tries to construct around their lives.

Karen too has been well trained by her mother: 'You were not made to leap in the dark either', Max tells her (*HP*: 142). Nevertheless her stay in Ireland alerts her to the danger of passive conformity and it is after she has slept with Max, and believes no one will ever find out, that Leopold comes into her thoughts: 'I am let back, safe, too safe … I shall die like Aunt Violet wondering what else there was' (*HP*: 152). A child would be permanent proof of her rebellion: 'He would be disaster … The street would stay torn up, the trams could not begin again' (*HP*: 154–5). When later Karen takes fright at her power to rebel, she has to reject Leopold who is part of that rebellion: 'He is more than a little boy. He is Leopold', she tells Ray (*HP*: 215). Marrying Ray, Karen covers over the fracture in their lives, employing against Leopold the same strategy of silence her mother had used against herself: 'No one knew about Leopold. The husk of silence round him was complete' (*HP*: 219).

In order to uncover the mystery of his origins, Leopold must break open the life in which he has been entombed by his mother's silence. Kathryn Johnson draws a parallel between the Anglo-Irish Big House and Mme Fisher's 'fatal house in Paris' with its isolation, mystery and a violent past that threatens Leopold's life in the present (Johnson, 2011: 214). Like his mother Leopold, suffocated by an overcontrolling upbringing, yearns to rebel: 'all the time he impressed them he despised them for being impressed; he wanted to crack the world by saying some final and frightful thing' (*HP*: 34). After reading Marian Grant Moody's fussy letter outlining the restrictive protocols that govern his life, as Lois pictures Danielstown in flames and Sydney hordes of Saracens descending on the hotel, so Leopold imagines a destructive wind blowing through their house in Spezia:

If he could have been re-embodied, at that moment a black wind would have rushed through the Villa Fioretta, wrenching the shutters off and tearing the pictures down, or an earthquake cracked the floors, or the olivey hill above the villa erupted, showering hot, choking ash (*HP*: 45).

Andrew Bennett and Nicholas Royle note: 'What both Leopold and his mother Karen simultaneously desire and dread ... are gashes, cracks, cuts in the order and propriety of social relationships' (Bennett and Royle, 1995: 48).

Leopold's fanatical need for his mother and for a place to belong stretches across the lengthy middle section in which her absence is explained. Critical readings of *The House in Paris* stress the damage inflicted on Leopold by adults covering up his origins. For Bennett and Royle, the scars on his neck and knee turn the novel into 'a traumaturgy, both a work and a theory of wounds' (Bennett and Royle, 1995: 43). Neil Corcoran describes the passage in which Leopold sobs, leaning against the very mantelpiece that witnessed his father cut his wrists, while Henrietta, for whom his tears possibly reawaken her own grief at her mother's death, knows not to offer consolation but simply moves towards him and weeps with him, as 'the novel's most concentrated expression of the psychological and emotional wounding that is parentlessness' (Corcoran, 2004: 83).

Critical opinion is undecided, however, over the role played at the end of the novel by Mme Fisher who, through sheer will power stays alive long enough to instruct Leopold as to his future. Lorna Wilkinson (Wilkinson, 2018: 7–8) discusses the Hansel and Gretel fairy story that permeates this episode: 'See me as so much gingerbread', Mme Fisher tells Leopold (*HP*: 200). Maud Ellmann suggests that Mme Fisher liberates Leopold by talking to him about his birth and adoption and imbuing him with a sense of his exceptional nature (Ellmann, 2004: 120). Kathryn Johnson reads this episode as Mme Fisher, like the witch in Grimms' fairy tale, setting a destructive trap for Leopold as she inculcates in him, through the image of his mother signing him away to the Grant Moodys 'like any puppy or kitten' (*HP*: 206), enough ideas to wreak havoc for years to come in his relationship with Karen (Johnson, 2011: 218).

Blocked in her mothering, Karen cannot face Leopold and the resolution is brought about by Ray, that apparently quintessential Englishman, who turns out to contravene the stereotype, being not quite the 'plain man' she had supposed (*HP*: 85). Loving Karen more perhaps because she has revealed herself capable of passion and courage, if not with him, Ray remains haunted by the thought of Karen's abandoned child. Corcoran likens the circular dialogue in Part III between Ray and Karen concerning Leopold to the 'Circe' episode of Joyce's *Ulysses* (Corcoran, 2004: 86). The novel ends with a second taxi ride as Ray and Leopold deliver Henrietta, who has crossed Paris but not seen anything of it, to her chaperone at the Gare de Lyon. Characteristic of Bowen, the ending is inconclusive: like the refugees that were soon to pour through European railway stations, Ray and Leopold remain poised for flight outside the Gare de Lyon as Ray fantasises about the liberation inherent in continental travel, thus providing an 'alternative transnational narrative' (Pearson, 2015: 97) to the menacing nationalisms of 1930s Europe. Rescuing a part Jewish child from fascist Europe Ray not only challenges social taboos which, as the novel demonstrates, still operated strongly against the adulterous woman and the illegitimate child, but he is also breaking the law, making their future not entirely straightforward. Nor do we know whether Karen will find the courage to overcome her ambivalence towards Leopold.

The question, probably unanswerable by this stage, is to what extent, during a period when the discourse allying women with motherhood was particularly virulent, Bowen's own emotions are reflected in the novel's poignant passages evoking a marriage haunted by childlessness, '[t]hat third chair left pushed in at a table set for a couple' (*HP*: 219). The period of composition of *The House in Paris* coincided with Bowen's first known love affair, with the literary scholar, Humphry House. During the course of this, a row blew up prompted, she later admitted in a letter dated July 1935, by her jealousy of Madeline House's pregnancy (Laurence, 2019: 139). Much has been excised from Bowen's correspondence with Ritchie but in one letter, dated 1957, she briefly allows herself to acknowledge 'yearning' after other people's children (*LCW*: 281). Adoption might have been an option but adoption always ends in failure in Bowen's fiction and a very forceful case is made against it in this novel through Leopold's feelings about the Grant Moodys: 'Have they bought me, or what?' (*HP*: 204). Similar unanswered questions around childlessness and adoption will haunt Bowen's next novel, *The Death of the Heart*, portrait of a young person who, like Leopold, forces the adult world to take account of her needs.

The Death of the Heart (1938)

In her 1942 interview for *The Bell*, Bowen declared:

> I regard myself as an Irish novelist. As long as I can remember, I've been extremely conscious of being Irish – even when I was writing about very un-Irish things such as suburban life in Paris or the English seaside (Foster, 1995: 118).

The choice of subjects here, suburban life in Paris and the English seaside, suggest she was thinking specifically of *The House in Paris* and *The Death of the Heart*, and in 'Anna', an unfinished story that may have been the genesis of *The Death of the Heart*, Anna is in fact Anglo-Irish (Johnson, 2011: 220–1). Apart from the Yeatsian swans of the opening paragraph, no trace of Anna's Irishness remains in the finished novel. Nevertheless the existence of this manuscript suggests that there may have been parallels in Bowen's mind between the Anglo-Irish as a class which employed bravado to conceal insecurity and even trauma, and her dissection of the unease and bad faith underlying the apparent complacencies of the English upper-middle classes. Matchett, the guardian of diurnal rituals and the Quayne family history, seems more like a servant in an Anglo-Irish Big House than in a 1930s London home – the reference to 'big houses' (*DH*: 73) is telling – while, like the younger generation of Anglo-Irish, Eddie and Portia, are heirs to a fallen world: 'How can we grow up when there's nothing left to inherit …?' Eddie asks (*DH*: 275).

More clearly than the Michaelis household, Thomas and Anna Quayne and their friends recognise that as a class they are on their way out. In this 'low dishonest decade' (W. H. Auden, 'September 1, 1939'), which witnessed the growth of the trade union movement and a series of hunger marches culminating in the 1936 Jarrow March, Thomas anticipates a working class revolution: 'The most we can hope is to go on getting away with it till the others get it away from us' (*DH*: 94). At the same time, Thomas sees justice in the ending of this society ruled by 'self-interest given a pretty gloss' (*DH*: 90). Inherited income from his mother has allowed him to take advantage of the newly developed advertising industry, while Anna's money has enabled her failed experiment in interior design, both very 1930s commercial activities that benefit from the increased leisure during the interwar period (Corcoran, 2004: 102; Stevenson, 1990: 381–411). That this commercially driven society has no place for and would rather forget about those post-war, post-imperial hangovers like Irene who returns from China impoverished and Major Brutt, ex manager of a failed rubber plantation in Malay, makes Thomas think the worse of his world: 'Major Brutt's being (frankly) a discard put the final blot on a world Thomas did not like' (*DH*: 90).

Thomas recognises that their patronage of the working-class young man, twenty-three-year-old Eddie, may well make the latter furious. Eddie, 'the brilliant child of an obscure home' (*DH*: 62), who has studied at Oxford, encounters a society so frozen in its class structures that, despite his cleverness, it is unable to treat him as anything other than as a 'striking turn' (*DH*: 62). Although seemingly prepared to play along, in reality Eddie burns with self-loathing and resentment: 'something abstract and lasting about the residue of his anger had been known, once or twice, to command respect' (*DH*: 62). His satirical novel has offended many who might have been his patrons but Thomas reads it with sympathy, acknowledging that Eddie has been free to say things about their world that he himself, more deeply embedded in society, cannot. Urged on by Anna, who wishes to put Eddie in his place after his unmeaning kiss, Thomas employs him in his firm on a three months' trial, fuelling Eddie's resentment at being financially obliged to accept his favour. In this, Eddie contrasts with Matchett who, with a greater sense of her own worth and more of a respect for her work, rules out subservience to her employers, refusing to flatter the first Mrs Quayne and taking 'suggestions only' from Anna (*DH*: 24). The coming democratic revolution, brought to fruition in the post-war Labour government under Clement Attlee, is prefigured in the class resentment of both Eddie and Daphne against Anna, and in Bowen's innovation in making the servant, Matchett, the ethical centre of *The Death of the Heart*, allowing her interior monologue to conclude the book.

The tripartite structure of *The Death of the Heart*, the titles of the three parts echoing the Christian litany, 'From all the deceits of the world, the flesh and the devil, Good Lord deliver us', emphasises the class theme. In Part One, 'the world' is represented in the stagey, unconvivial atmosphere of Thomas and Anna's Regent's Park Nash house, 2 Windsor Terrace, with its segregated living areas – Anna's chilly drawing room, Thomas's fumy downstairs study, Matchett's secret basement, Portia's bedroom. In such an atmosphere – 'The rooms were set for strangers' intimacy, or else for exhausted solitary retreat' (*DH*: 42) – St Quentin, the Quaynes' family friend who detests intimacy, fits right in, whereas Thomas's genuine passion for Anna, awakened since their marriage, finds no room to express itself. In 'The Forgotten Art of Living' (1948), Bowen commented: 'We think out our interiors (spacing, lighting and colour), but then dread to feel them' (*PPT*: 395). Ritchie noted accurately in his diary that 2 Windsor Terrace was 'an exact description' of Bowen's Regent's Park home, that Thomas Quayne was 'an unsparing portrait' of Alan Cameron and that Eddie was based on Goronwy Rees with whom Bowen had had a failed love affair (*LCW*: 25). Ritchie plausibly read Anna and Portia as two halves of Bowen herself, Anna being Bowen seen from the outside as a stylish, socially capable adult woman, while Portia, he said, in an insight that tells us much about the vulnerabilities of the adult Bowen, was 'the hidden E who I have got to know through love' (*LCW*: 26).

A cataclysm opens up in Anna's carefully constructed world when, in a situation Bowen likened to Maria Edgeworth's novels (*LCW*: 26), sixteen-year-old Portia, Thomas' orphaned stepsister, arrives to stay. Portia is an unfortunate reminder to Thomas of his father's embarrassing second marriage, while her doomed love for Eddie reawakens Anna's memories of her lengthy affair with the ex-soldier, Robert Pidgeon, that ended cruelly for her. Failures in her career as an interior designer and in her hopes of becoming a mother (she has had two miscarriages) have resulted in Anna's defensive text for her life that requires a worldly, sophisticated mind to read it with any sympathy. Portia's blindly literal reading innocently exposes Anna's limitations. 'I don't say it has changed the course of my life, but it's given me a rather more disagreeable feeling about being alive – or, at least, about being me', she confesses, after snooping on Portia's diary (*DH*: 304). Neither she nor Thomas can rise to the text of family life Portia has prepared for them: 'She makes me feel like a tap that won't turn on' (*DH*: 246). In an interview, Bowen called *The Death of the Heart* 'a tragedy of atrophy', with Portia being 'the awake one' (*LI*: 279).

Writing and telling stories, as Harriet Chessman has observed, equates with power in this novel (Chessman, 1983). In the opening scene Anna, recounting to St Quentin old Mr Quayne's love affair with Irene and Portia's birth, writes Portia into a text that is both demeaning and farcical. Portia's father is presented as an overgrown schoolboy gone to seed and her mother as a vulgar little thing, their love affair 'one of those muddles without a scrap of dignity' (*DH*: 16). In Anna's tale of their wandering exile in shabby hotels and villas up and down the Riviera, their dignity is undermined in every possible way until even St Quentin is led to exclaim that her story curdles his blood. When he eventually meets Portia he questions Anna's text: 'What a high forehead she's got … I wonder where she got that distinction. From what you say, her mother was quite a mess' (*DH*: 30). Anna's unreliable narrative of Portia's parents is rewritten by Matchett who, full of 'vexed ambition for Portia' (*DH*: 22), recognises the girl as rightful heir to Windsor Terrace and rescues Portia's father from Anna's patronising account. Irene's story is later retold in a different way, through Portia's loving memories of their life together.

Like Bowen's other young women – Lois in *The Last September*, Theodora in *Friends and Relations* – the ever-watchful Portia yearns to write herself into the script of adult life. In order to do so she has to learn to read the complex text of life at Windsor Terrace where 'people said what they did not mean, and did not say what they meant' (*DH*: 59). To Portia, Eddie presents himself as natural, open and naïve. He is not: 'his apparent rushes of Russian frankness proved, when you came to look back at them later, to have been more carefully edited than you had known at the time' (*DH*: 62). But Portia has no experience to go on in reading Eddie and, in trusting that he will be able to replace the intimacy she experienced with her mother, Portia misreads him completely. At the end of the novel, she walks around Eddie's room giving 'the impression of being someone who, having lost their way in a book or mistaken its whole import, has to go back and start from the beginning again' (*DH*: 277).

Nothing in Portia's previous life has prepared her for this kind of text. The intense, symbiotic relationship she had with Irene, mirroring the close relationship between Bowen and her mother after they relocated to England (*MT*: 279), has left Portia, for the purposes of understanding upper-middle-class English life, illiterate:

> Untaught, they had walked arm-in-arm along city pavements, and at nights had pulled their beds closer together or slept in the same bed – overcoming, as far as might be, the separation of birth. Seldom had they faced up to society – when they did, Irene did the wrong thing, then cried (*DH*: 56).

The fashionable girls' school to which Anna sends Portia highlights Irene's ignorance of the rules of this society:

> Irene herself – knowing that nine out of ten things you do direct from the heart are the wrong thing, and that she was not capable of doing anything better – would not have dared to cross the threshold of this room (*DH*: 56).

Portia, however, has to cross the threshold. Ill-prepared as she is, she has no choice but to leave behind the close, symbiotic relationship with her mother and join the adult world of language and civilisation, 'the world in which she had to live' (*DH*: 29).

The truth of Portia's language in her diary, more direct than that used by Anna and her friends, is attested to by St Quentin, the novelist:

> I swear that each of us keeps, battened down inside himself, a sort of lunatic giant – impossible socially, but full-scale – and that it's the knockings and batterings we sometimes hear in each other that keeps our intercourse from utter banality. Portia hears these the whole time; in fact she hears nothing else (*DH*: 310).

Portia's struggle to find her voice reflects Bowen's own life. Displaced as a child, shunted as an adolescent between relatives' homes, Bowen commented: 'My writing, I am prepared to think, may be a substitute for something I have been born without – a so-called normal relation to society' (*MT*: 223). Reading Rider Haggard's novel, *She*, was a turning point: '*writing* ... what it could do! That was the revelation; that was the power in the cave ... The power of the pen' (*MT*: 250). Like Portia, Bowen found in writing the grown-up status for which she yearned:

> Motherless since I was thirteen, I was in and out of the homes of my different relatives ... Though quite happy, I lived with a submerged fear that I might fail to establish grown-up status. That fear, it may be, egged me on to writing ... As far as I now see, I must have been anxious to approximate to my elders, yet to demolish them (*MT*: 121).

The verb 'demolish' is telling in the context of the generational power struggle between Portia and Anna as to whose story will prevail: 'it's really a struggle for ascendancy', Bowen commented in 1959 (*LI*: 332).

Anna is the only person who could help Portia interpret the text of adult life correctly, as is made clear in the middle section of the novel, 'The Flesh'. Here, mirroring Fanny Price's downward trajectory in *Mansfield Park*, Portia is packed off to stay with Anna's former governess, Mrs Heccomb, at Seale-on-Sea, a version of Hythe where, as a young girl, Bowen had lived with her mother. Even in this seemingly frank and casual lower-middle-class Waikiki household that feels more like the life she was accustomed to with Irene, there are conventions, prudish ones, which Portia unwittingly contravenes when she mentions Eddie's handholding to Daphne, whose hand he had been holding. Portia disrupts the Waikiki household as much as she unsettles Windsor Terrace by failing to understand their codes of behaviour.

Portia's stay at Waikiki marks, however, a turning-point in her relationship with Anna when, prompted by Mrs Heccomb's sentimental portrait of the twelve-year-old motherless Anna, Portia dreams she is sharing a book with Anna as a little girl. The dream registers Anna's refusal to help Portia 'read' life but it also leaves Portia with a feeling of guilt that 'she had not been kind to Anna' (*DH*: 141). The dream prompts Portia to cease judging Anna, or at least, in the words of Shakespeare's heroine, to temper justice with mercy as she begins to understand that the withholding, cauterising older woman may once have had her own vulnerabilities: 'Had Anna felt small at day school? ... Did Anna also, sometimes, not know what to do next?' (*DH*: 141).

Tolerance as a mark of maturity is underlined by Major Brutt, 'appendix to the finished story of Robert' (*DH*: 261). With his persistent illusions about Anna's cheerful family home, Major Brutt constitutes 'the same standing, or, better still, undermining reproach as Portia' (*DH*: 260). He suggests to Portia that she has been too stern a judge of Thomas and Anna. This is, in a sense, what everyone tells Portia in the final section of the novel, from Eddie ('My God, we've got to live in the world,' (*DH*: 282)) to St Quentin who tells her that it does not do to write things down just as they occur, facts must be glossed to protect others' feelings: 'if one didn't let oneself swallow some few lies, I don't know how one would ever carry the past' (*DH*: 249).

There is a cost to this. 'The Devil' (the title of the third section), is that, though writing her diary has given Portia power over the seriously rattled inhabitants of Windsor Terrace, she cannot enter the world of authorship without losing some of her innocence. As St Quentin remarks, innocence is lost the moment one picks up the pen: 'Style is the thing that's always a bit phony, and at the same time you cannot write without style' (*DH*: 11). However unvarnished Portia's style may seem, the very fact of writing entails untruth, 'polishing up' the facts: 'that's style', St Quentin comments admiringly of her placing of the comma in the first sentence in her diary (*DH*: 11). When Portia deliberately destroys Major Brutt's sentimental reading of Anna's life, 'the death of the heart' has already begun to set in for her. By the end of the novel, she has become thoroughly disabused, seeing her childhood through the eyes of Thomas and Anna, as funny and slightly despicable, and Eddie reneging on their shared private world. Her innocence, once lost, will be lost forever: 'This can't happen again', she tells Major Brutt (*DH*: 292). Portia cannot remain the little girl Matchett wishes; she must make her way through the world, the flesh and the devil in order to come to terms with the society in which she has to live. 'It is not only our fate but our business to lose innocence, and once we have lost that it is futile to attempt to picnic in Eden', Bowen once memorably said (*MT:* 50).

Portia agrees to give Anna and Thomas a second chance by setting them an ethical challenge, a test of the heart. That it takes the Quaynes so long to decide what to do shows how far removed their lives are from the spontaneous gesture. It is Anna who in the final scene goes some way to acknowledging Portia's viewpoint in her speech beginning: 'If I were Portia?' (*DH*: 312). And it is Anna who comes up with the solution of sending Matchett, guardian of the home, the furniture and the Quayne family history, to fetch Portia, thereby finally acknowledging Thomas's half-sister as rightful heir to Windsor Terrace. In performing this tentative renegotiation in their relations, Anna knows that their relationship will have no easy solution: 'I shall always insult her; she will always persecute me' (*DH*: 312–3).

Any home Portia finds with Anna and Thomas is likely to be transitory for the notion lingers in the background that after a year with the Quaynes she is to go abroad to her mother's sister. In Major Brutt's rackety lodgings in Kensington she resembles 'a refugee', the vocabulary evoking, like that around Max in *The House in Paris*, the ever menacing 1930s political context: 'unhappy on his bed, in this temporary little stale room, Portia seemed to belong nowhere, not even here' (*DH*: 293). Though *The Death of the Heart* concludes on a note of summer promise, the ending is never quite resolved. Matchett is arriving to fetch her but for the moment Portia remains 'displaced' in the Karachi Hotel, ending where she began life with her parents, in a cheap hotel room.

Betrayal is everywhere in *The Death of the Heart*. In Bowen's next novel, *The Heat of the Day* (1949), themes of spying and treachery will take on a political urgency, but before publication of that novel the war intervened, during which Bowen published some of her finest short stories, and it is to these we now turn.

CHAPTER FOUR

Short Stories

Interwar Stories

In a series of prefaces and reviews Bowen, one of the major short story writers of the twentieth century, reflected deeply on the form and her own practice of it. In her preface to a selection of her stories published in 1959 she suggested that one distinction between the novel and the short story was that the latter, being 'more concentrated' and 'more visionary' deals with a moment of crisis and looks deeper into the abyss: 'The short story, as I see it to be, allows for what is crazy about humanity: obstinacies, inordinate heroisms, "immortal longings"' (*MT*: 130). Bowen here joins a strand of critical thinking on the short story that views it as a liminal form exploring dreams, visions, hauntings and the unconscious, and therefore particularly suited to modernist concerns (May, 1994: 133). In doing so, Bowen was distancing herself from the Gaelic tradition of oral storytelling, as well as from the well-made story in the realist vein as practised, for example, by her contemporary, Frank O'Connor.

Bowen's stories are fragmented, inconclusive, and interested in states of mind. In her preface to *The Faber Book of Modern Short Stories* (1937), she described the short story as a modern art form and linked it with that other twentieth-century form, the cinema:

> The short story is a young art: as we now know it, it is the child of this century. Poetic tautness and clarity are so essential to it that it may be said to stand at the edge of prose; in its use

of action it is nearer to drama than to the novel. The cinema, itself busy with a technique, is of the same generation: in the last thirty years the two arts have been accelerating together (May, 1994: 256).

Bowen connected the short story with both the intensity of poetry – 'The story should have the valid central emotion and inner spontaneity of the lyric' – and with the immediacy of a painting – 'The story should be as composed, in the plastic sense, and as visual as a picture' (May, 1994: 260). Rather than relying on a discursive sequence of causes and effects, many of her stories end on a question:

> The short story, free from the *longueurs* of the novel, is also exempt from the novel's conclusiveness – too often forced and false: it may thus more nearly than the novel approach aesthetic and moral truth (May, 1994: 261).

Commenting on this open-endedness in her preface to *A Day in the Dark and Other Stories* (1965), she added: 'I can at least explain it by saying that I expect the reader to be as (reasonably) imaginative as myself' (Bowen, 1965: 9).

In 'The Short Story in England' (1945), Bowen traces the evolution of the modern short story from Kipling through Russian authors like Chekhov and French writers like Maupassant and Flaubert to Katherine Mansfield and D. H. Lawrence, all of whom in different ways influenced her own work. She briefly references Irish writers (James Joyce, Frank O'Connor, Sean O'Faoláin, Liam O'Flaherty) and in other critical writings discusses at length James Joyce whose *Dubliners* she particularly admired (see her review of Joyce's career published in *The Bell*, 1941). Her early stories in *Encounters* (1923) and *Ann Lee's* (1926) demonstrate from the start her willingness to explore modernist techniques, giving us inconclusive states of mind, free indirect discourse, the use of epiphanies and symbols as structuring devices, lack of closure and downplaying of plot in favour of mood and atmosphere. They already display some of Bowen's signature themes: the manipulative older woman ('Mrs Windermere'), an intimate mother-daughter relationship ('Coming Home'), moving house ('The New House'), home coming ('The Return'), the uncanny reappearance of the past ('The Shadowy Third'), childhood bereavement ('The Visitor'), instability of identity ('Human Habitation'), as well as the English abroad, chiefly in Italy ('Requiescat', 'The Contessina', 'The Secession', 'The Storm').

Bowen's 1949 preface to a new edition of *Encounters* describing the circumstances in which this first book was written, in an attic room in her aunt's house in Harpenden, is testament to the intense concentration and commitment she brought to her art:

> The room, the position of the window, the compulsive and anxious grating of my chair on the board floor were hyper-significant for me: here were sensuous witnesses to my crossing the margin of a hallucinatory world (*MT*: 118).

Bowen was writing in a vacuum, cut off from literary movements, in a form that had not yet differentiated itself from a sketch, and before she had read the work of Chekhov, Maupassant, James or Mansfield. Having failed in attempts at poetry and painting, Bowen aimed to carve a place for herself in the adult world through her stories. *Encounters* was well received and the following year she published her first novel but, unlike many authors who view the form as an apprenticeship, she never abandoned the short story.

The darkening subject matter and broadening social context that Bowen detected in the 1930s short story (*PPT*: 312–13) are already evident in certain stories from her 1920s collections, *Ann Lee's* (1926) and *Joining Charles* (1929). 'Recent Photograph', for example, reflects the period's growing obsession with high profile crimes and their sensationalist reporting in the newspapers as Bertram Lukin, a journalist with the *Evening Crier*, hunts for copy from neighbours in the Brindley murder case. The life of Mr Brindley, who has cut his wife's throat then gassed himself, has become public property but Lukin, searching for 'a bit of colour' that will give him the edge over rival journalists, decides to emphasise Mrs Brindley's youth: 'Nothing went so well in a headline as a Young Wife – except, of course, a Bride or a Girl Mother' (*CS*: 216). Later he meets a local teenager, Verbena, who informs him of another element in the story – Mr Brindley had recently lost his job and tried to conceal this from his domineering wife who discovered the truth on the day the crime was committed. Lukin revises his headline to 'Wife's Discovery Precipitates Tragedy of Disappointed Man' (*CS:* 219). Verbena shows him a recent photograph of Mr Brindley with sticking plaster on his lip, suggesting that there may be still more to be uncovered about the story but Lukin, who has to file his copy, does not stay to find out. Fixing the meaning of the photograph for his readers, he has missed the deeper story behind it: 'The whole truth was, for the purposes of his profession, a thing of too various dimensions to be easily encompassed' (*CS*: 217). Bowen's satirical story is a damning indictment of media distortions.

The growing popularity of cinema-going is explored by Bowen in 'Dead Mabelle' where she describes the uncanny emotional connection between a silent film star, the eponymous Mabelle, and her avid fan, bank clerk William Stickford, who becomes consumed by daydreams about the star to the point that his daily life begins to feel unreal and he is reprimanded at work for 'excessive cinema-going' (*CS*: 280). Bowen is at pains to emphasise that even before his cinema-going William's sense of self is fragile, undermined by his random reading of philosophy in a lonely bid, like that of E. M. Forster's Leonard Bast, to educate himself out of his class. Mabelle's sudden death in a mysterious fire is transformed into a marketing opportunity and the story explores film's uncanny ability to give an after-life to someone who is dead:

'You're more here than I...' William reflects, viewing Mabelle's final posthumous film (*CS*: 284). He contemplates suicide but the banal contents of his drawer, containing notebooks, a pencil stump and match-ends where there should have been a pistol, deny him a filmic ending and bring him back to everyday life. 'Dead Mabelle' is a warning to cinema-goers of the dangers of allowing themselves to be caught up in a false sense of intimacy with its stars. Though Bowen appears to criticize, or even mock, William, in a later essay 'Why I Go To the Cinema' (1938), she admits to not being immune herself to enjoying this uncanny feeling of connection with cinematic stars: 'how seldom in real life (or so-called real life) does acquaintanceship, much less intimacy, with dazzling, exceptional beings come one's way?' (*LI*: 198).

'Dead Mabelle' illustrates how in the early twentieth century new technological inventions (the telephone, telegraph, radio, film) could seem to have something magical about them to people who did not understand the science behind them (Beer, 1996: 149–66). Following on from Pamela Thurschwell's exploration of the intersection of literary culture, the occult, psychoanalysis and new technology in a period when psychical research was not yet clearly separated from scientific (Thurschwell, 2001), Sinéad Mooney links the ghost theme in Bowen's writing to 'a modern world perceived as fractured, dislocated, precarious' (Mooney, 2009a: 78). This is borne out by Bowen's 1952 preface to *The Second Ghost Book* edited by Cynthia Asquith where Bowen, who once declared that she believed in 'God *and* ghosts' (Glendinning, 1978: 297), traces the link between ghosts and contemporary interest in trauma and disturbed states of mind:

> On the whole, it would seem they adapt themselves well, perhaps better than we do, to changing world conditions – they enlarge their domain, shift their hold on our nerves and, dispossessed of one habitat, set up house in another ... They know how to curdle electric light, chill off heating, or

de-condition air. Long ago they captured railway trains and installed themselves in liners' luxury cabins; now telephones, motors, planes and radio wavelengths offer them self-expression. The advance of psychology has gone their way; the guilt complex is their especial friend. Ghosts have grown up (*AFT*: 101).

She drew explicit connections between the short story form and supernatural themes in her notes for lectures she gave in 1960 to Vassar College students:

> The UNCANNY means – I think? – the unknowable – something beyond the bounds of *rational* knowledge –
> In this I include the GHOST STORY – with its content of *fear*.
> With *Fear*, we return to *Primitive Feeling*.
> The Short Story can *depict* or *evoke fear*.
> The extent to which it involves *us* in the *primitive sense of fear* is the measure of the "Success" of the Ghost STORY (*B*: 15–16).

In 'Foothold' where Janet's suppressed boredom and dissatisfaction in her marriage manifests itself in the ghost, Clara, recipient of confidences Janet cannot share with her husband, the ghost as projection of a psychological state, the female bonding and domestic setting are all characteristic of what Diana Wallace terms 'suburban Gothic' (Wallace, 2004: 63), and what Bowen herself referred to as 'those uneasy currents beneath the apparently placid surface' characteristic of the interwar short story (*PPT*: 314). The theme of domestic unease is heightened in 'Attractive Modern Homes', where her new house on one of the middle-class housing estates that sprang up during the interwar years already feels haunted to Mrs Watson, caught in a no-place when old habits are disrupted and new ones have not yet formed. 'In our seeing of ghosts, each of us has exposed our susceptibilities, which are partly personal, partly those of our own time', Bowen declared, emphasising that while her ghost stories may focus on the domestic, like her novels they are always related to wider cultural and political contexts, here the dislocations brought about by interwar building programmes (*AFT*: 104).

As the 1930s progressed, Bowen detected a change in the short story form:

> The tenseness and seriousness of that decade, in which England could not ignore the troubles of Europe or the storm clouds darkening her own horizon, began to reflect itself in our short stories ... Social consciousness succeeded to aesthetic susceptibility. The general feeling that we must begin to act brought action back into prominence in our stories. Charming descriptive passages yielded place to quick-moving dialogue; and characters, instead of being poetically generalised, had to be clear-cut, perhaps prosaic, identifiable by the reader as types in everyday life (*PPT*: 312–13).

In this decade, Bowen's short stories, even more than her novels, became the place where she plunged into trauma: murder in 'The Cat Jumps', 'Reduced' and 'The Disinherited', child suicide and post-traumatic stress disorder in 'The Apple Tree', a seamstress seduced then abandoned, eking out life as a single mother in 'The Needlecase', the difficulty of finding money for an abortion in 'Firelight in the Flat'. There was a widening of the social scene so that in 'The Disinherited', a story that moves between a freezing country house, a stuffy manor house and a featureless home on an unfinished housing estate, middle-class Marianne's boredom is set in the context of the stultifying domestic ideology that dominated interwar Britain (D'hoker, 2012: 267–89) and is juxtaposed to the bitterness of an impoverished younger generation of gentry 'stranded' between the old order which prepared them for privilege and the new in which they can find no role. Bowen's 1930s stories continue her critique of the tabloid newspapers' obsession with sensational reporting of high profile crimes such as the trial of Patrick Mahon in 1924 for murdering and dismembering his mistress which finds echoes in Prothero's story in 'The Disinherited' and in 'The Cat Jumps' (Stewart, 2009: 139–59).

'The Cat Jumps' is set in 'Rose Hill', a suburban English house, scene of Harold Bentley's murder and dismemberment of his wife, dubbed by the tabloids '*The Rose Hill Horror*'. Through her depiction of the new owners, the ironically named Wrights, who are up to date in psychoanalysis, displaying for their guests books by Freud, Krafft-Ebing, and 'the heterosexual volume' of Havelock Ellis, Bowen indicates the original links between psychoanalysis and the supernatural, and suggests the inadequacy of psychology to withstand the more disturbing aspects of life. The modern, sceptical generation of the Wrights and their friends are determined not to believe in hauntings but the supernatural creeps in anyway as the horror intensifies through a series of ghost story tropes: the stormy night, an unexplained smell (identified as the dead woman's perfume), and outbreaks of what Bowen calls 'sex-antagonism' that affect even the children and the servants. As often in her supernatural stories, unease shades into downright hostility between the sexes: Mr Wright perceives his wife as suffocating while Jocelyn Wright, like the other women in the story, becomes increasingly terrified by the thought of male violence. The story ends on a mixture of horror and farce as Harold Wright, whose first name doubles with that of the murderer, steps out of the bathroom and Jocelyn faints through sheer terror at this apparent reincarnation of Harold Bentley.

In 'Look at All Those Roses', Lou finds herself drawn to a house where a murder may have been committed. The story begins realistically enough with a tetchy modern couple's car breaking down as they drive through the countryside. It turns into a mythical, dreamlike story resembling a fairy tale when Lou, waiting for Edward to return with a garage mechanic, finds herself taken over by the disturbing yet empowering female world of Mrs Mather and her thirteen-year-old daughter, Josephine. Josephine lies immobile in an invalid carriage, her back injured by her father six years previously, since when he has not been seen. Lou, drawn into the pre-oedipal, timeless world of mother and daughter, lies down sleepily with Josephine amidst the overpowering scent of the roses in the Mathers' garden. Hypnotized by the abundant hallucinatory roses which come to possess such a sinister quality that she wonders whether they are being fertilized by Mr Mather's corpse, Lou surrenders her rational consciousness to a dreamlike intuition of past events, which might include Mr Mather's murder, before being brought back to clock time by the arrival of Edward in a hurry to rescue her from the house. In her fine analysis of this story, Maud Ellmann remarks on 'the collision between genres' in 'Look At All Those Roses', between 'the urbanity of social comedy' in Lou's scenes with Edward and 'the oneiric landscapes of the fairytale' in the Mathers' garden (Ellmann, 2004: 4). With its uncanny atmosphere, hints of female violence, a possibly murdered husband, and a disturbed young girl, 'Look At All Those Roses' contains echoes of Katherine Mansfield's 'The Woman at the Store', a story Bowen much admired, as she did all of Mansfield's work in the short story (Ingman, 2018: 30–41).

Children continue to feature in Bowen's stories from this period: children alone together acting on one another in 'Charity' and 'The Jungle', recalling passages in *The House in Paris*; damaged children like Frederick in 'Tears, Idle Tears' and Henrietta in 'The Easter Egg Party', who destroys the spinsters' faith in childhood innocence; the little rich girl acting up in a vicarage family setting in 'Maria', an autobiographical story (*MT*: 273–4) which is a prototype for *Eva Trout*; the motherless Geraldine, farmed out to her step-grandmother who turns her into an experiment in child-rearing in 'The Little Girl's Room', a story that challenges the notion, so prevalent in interwar media, that all women are naturally fitted for motherhood. Clara Ellis exclaims: '"Women

– how they ever bring up their own children!" Mrs Letherton-Channing pulled off one or two dead roses. "Look how they fail", she said placidly' (*CS*: 430), a doubly ironic judgement in view of her own failure properly to nurture Geraldine.

Interwar Ireland

In 'The Back Drawing-Room' (1926), Bowen moves from a discussion about immortality, spiritualism and telepathy among a group of London sophisticates into an older tradition of Irish Protestant supernatural fiction found in the work of Charles Maturin, Sheridan Le Fanu, Bram Stoker and W. B. Yeats and focused on the Big House. A central argument of W. J. McCormack's pioneering study, *Dissolute Characters* (1993), is that nineteenth-century Irish writers like Le Fanu anticipated the psychic dislocations characteristic of modernist writers. Bowen was a perceptive reader of Le Fanu, as her preface to *Uncle Silas* demonstrates and, sharing Le Fanu's sense of anxiety over the rapidly vanishing Anglo-Irish class, she was influenced by his use of the ghost story to articulate social and psychological anxieties about the Anglo-Irish in her fiction.

In 'The Back Drawing-Room', the English interlocutors combine to try to silence the stranger who insists on lowering the conversation from sophisticated abstractions to the level of a ghost story based on his own experience during a recent stay in Ireland. Undeterred, the stranger recounts his Irish adventure in a manner that reveals lingering English ignorance as he transforms Ireland's recent war of independence and civil war into 'these civic disturbances' (*CS*: 203). Describing how, in search of somewhere to repair his bicycle, he came across a large demesne, he at last succeeds in attracting the attention of his listeners who attempt to add literary touches to his story from their reading of Gothic literature, all of which are refuted by the determinedly prosaic narrator. When he enters the back drawing room, he finds a young lady sobbing as if her world has ended. Knowing he can do nothing for her, he retreats, as the English had recently retreated from Ireland, leaving the Anglo-Irish to their own devices. Later the narrator learns that the house was Kilbarran, an Anglo-Irish house burnt down by the rebels two years previously. A familiar Bowen theme, the rootlessness of the dispossessed, is introduced: the Barran family may be still alive in Dublin or England, but it hardly matters where they are since they can no longer be at home, they have become living ghosts. The narrator is quietly bundled away and the room falls silent, suggesting English guilt at having abandoned the Anglo-Irish to their fate.

'Her Table Spread' presents another Anglo-Irish house on the brink of dissolution for, if Valeria Cuffe, the statuesque, simple-minded Anglo-Irish heiress and last of her line, fails to marry, her aunt fears that the castle will have to be sold and the family scattered. To prevent this, an Englishman, Alban, has been invited over to make a match with Miss Cuffe. Alban, like Thomas in 'Foothold' or St Quentin in *The Death of the Heart*, is one of Bowen's Jamesian hangers-on, a detached observer who remains negative about women and is convinced that the Anglo-Irish are all mad. The intensity and isolation of the Anglo-Irish way of life, described by Bowen in *Bowen's Court*, is revealed in the fantasy Valeria has woven around English officers who once visited the castle in her absence. Valeria takes little notice of Alban, her imagination being absorbed by these English officers whose arrival she expects at any moment due to the presence of an English destroyer in the estuary. In *Bowen's Court*, Bowen likened life in the Anglo-Irish Big House to 'a continuous, semi-physical dream' (*BC*: 451) and in 'Her Table Spread', the Anglo-Irish heiress, who relies on the English to save her, sums up in her person the hopeless political fantasies of her class. As in 'The Back Drawing-Room', the English disappoint: the English officers do not turn up, Alban is not attracted to Valeria. There is a moment, though, when Alban abandons egocentricity sufficiently to acknowledge the splendour of Valeria and her relatives:

Close by, Valeria's fingers creaked on her warm wet satin. She laughed like a princess, magnificently justified. Their unseen faces were all three lovely, and, in the silence after the laughter, such strong tenderness reached him that, standing there in full manhood, he was for a moment not exiled (*CS*: 424).

Taken together, 'The Back Drawing-Room' and 'Her Table Spread' suggest that the English should both acknowledge their guilt towards the Anglo-Irish and, like Alban, appreciate the bravado of a social performance sustained through a time of crisis. Conversely, 'The Tommy Crans', in which two children, the adopted Nancy and the fatherless Herbert, form a bond against irresponsible adults, indicts the extravagance of an earlier generation of Anglo-Irish.

Wartime Stories

War was ideal literary territory for Bowen, allowing her to deal with moments when the surface of civilised life cracks. She believed that the short story was better able than other forms to register the immediate impact of war since novels required lengthier gestation whereas the short story writer, like the poet:

> … gains rather than loses by being close up to what is immediately happening … Wartime London – blitzed, cosmopolitan, electric with expectation – teemed, I feel, with untold but tellable stories; glittered with scenes that cry aloud for the pen (*PPT*: 315).

During the war, Bowen published two short story collections, *Look At All Those Roses* (1941), which contains four war stories, and her finest collection, *The Demon Lover* (1945). In her postscript to the latter she described these wartime stories, written between the spring of 1941 and late autumn of 1944, as 'flying particles of something enormous and inchoate that had been going on. They were sparks from an experience – an experience not necessarily my own' (*MT*: 95). The suggestion that war is not an individual, but a general, experience runs through Bowen's war stories ('They are the particular. But through the particular, in wartime, I felt the high-voltage current of the general pass' (*MT*: 99)) and is aptly illustrated by 'In the Square', the first story in *The Demon Lover*. 'In the Square' shows the war opening up fractures in people's lives, causing them to live in ways they would not have done had it not been for the war, with classes, generations, mistresses and wives mixed up in a single London house: 'Who would think that this was the same world?' reflects Magdala, the owner of the house, two years into the war (*CS*: 611). Bowen commented on the democratisation brought about by the bombing:

> The violent destruction of solid things, the explosion of the illusion that prestige, power and permanence attach to bulk and weight, left all of us, equally, heady and disembodied. Walls went down; and we felt, if not knew, each other (*MT*: 95).

During wartime, with lives at the mercy of German bombardments and government restrictions, dreams and fantasies, Bowen argued, constituted a form of resistance: 'Dreams by night, and the fantasies – these often childishly innocent – with which formerly matter-of-fact people consoled themselves by day were compensations' (*MT*: 96). 'To survive, not only physically but spiritually, was essential' (*MT*: 97). For Pepita, the young woman in one of Bowen's most powerful stories, 'Mysterious Kôr', moonlit bombed out London conjures up visions of Kôr, the ancient abandoned city in Rider Haggard's *She*, the novel that in childhood had inspired Bowen with a sense of what writing could do. Forced by the overcrowded conditions of wartime London to wander through the city with her soldier lover, Pepita's means of self-preservation in the midst of war is to dream of Kôr: 'if you can blow whole places out of existence, you can blow whole places into it', she insists (*CS*: 730).

'Mysterious Kôr' illustrates what Bowen called 'those interior fairy tales (sometimes, perhaps, ridiculous; often touching) on which men and women sustain themselves and keep their identities throughout the cataclysm of world war' (*PPT*: 314).

At a time when homes and with them entire ways of life were being blown up, identity was fractured and personality became peculiarly porous as war dissolved psychic as well as social boundaries: 'the overcharged subconsciousnesses of everybody overflowed and merged' (*MT*: 95). Bowen employed ghost themes to convey the uncanniness of wartime experience in stories such as 'Pink May', 'Green Holly', 'The Cheery Soul' and most notably in 'The Demon Lover' where a soldier killed in the First World War comes back in the Second to haunt his former fiancée who has since married. As Mrs Drover's soldier fiancé takes her on a nightmarish and seemingly unending taxi drive through London, 'The Demon Lover' captures the eeriness of life during the Blitz, the suffocation of obsessive love and, in the feeling that the violence of the First World War is starting over again, an echo of Freud's uncanny repetition.

The First World War is also unfinished business for the nameless young woman in 'Songs My Father Sang Me' who, in a wartime encounter in a bar, hears a song from the previous war that reminds her of her father and his inability, like Major Brutt in *The Death of the Heart* and Prothero in 'The Disinherited', to find a place for himself in England after the war. 'Songs My Father Sang Me' is one of a series of Bowen stories in which pressures of war induce a return to scenes of childhood trauma. The sudden disappearance of her father who is not, it turns out, her biological father, on her seventh birthday has left the young woman fixated on his memory and, like many other Bowen characters, damaged by mysteries around her birth.

Arrested childhood and the First World War feature in another masterly story, 'Ivy Gripped the Steps', in which Gavin Doddington, on leave from the Ministry, returns to the seaside town of Southstone in 1944 after the official ban on visitors has been lifted, as the writer Bertram returns in 'The Lost Hope' (1946) and as Bowen described her own return to wartime Hythe in 'By the Unapproachable Sea' (1944) (*PPT*: 56–8). Gavin, child of a farming family in the English Midlands whose struggles, as Maud Ellmann notes, contain distinct echoes of Anglo-Irish impoverishment (Ellmann, 2004: 147), is sent to stay for his health with the wealthy Mrs Nicholson in Southstone in the years immediately preceding the First World War. His eight-year-old enjoyment of Southstone, its ease, prosperity and gaudy architecture, echoes Bowen's delight in the newness and gaiety of the south coast on moving to England with her mother in 1906 (*MT*: 277–81), but Gavin's growing love for Mrs Nicholson and consequent sense of rivalry with Admiral Concannon come to an abrupt halt with his discovery that Mrs Nicholson has used him for company, as one might 'a little dog' (*CS*: 707). This cruel discovery has so crippled his capacity for love that he has become a promiscuous 'amorist' (*CS*: 689), strangled by his past with Mrs Nicholson as her house is being strangled by ivy.

If Gavin, looking into the past, finds 'a whole stopped mechanism for feeling' (*CS;* 711), in 'The Inherited Clock' childhood bullying develops into Clara's trauma around time that has been suppressed until now. As with Gavin whose wartime return to Southstone recalls what he has now learned to term, after Proust, '*l'horreur de mon néant*' (*CS*: 710), so the inherited clock triggers off in Clara terrifying awareness of the emptiness of the past nine years of her life waiting for Henry to leave his wife. In such stories Bowen depicts war as a period when the surface cracks and suppressed traumas are brought to the surface: 'The past, in all these cases, discharges its load of feeling into the anaesthetized and bewildered present', she wrote in her postscript to *The Demon Lover* (*MT*: 98).

Other stories paint a general picture of life in wartime London. 'Careless Talk' satirises the self-importance of Londoners left behind in the city, pretending to know more than they do about wartime matters, while 'The Dolt's Tale' depicts wartime profiteering.

In 'Oh Madam', set in a bombed-out London house, Bowen adopts the monologue form, much as Katherine Mansfield had in 'The Lady's Maid' (1920), to give a voice to a servant whose devotion is exploited by her employer.

Ireland in Wartime

For an Anglo-Irish writer like Bowen the war posed a conflict of loyalty. Whilst feeling it was her duty to support the war effort by spending the majority of the war years in London, Bowen understood that Ireland's neutrality was, as she observed in her reports for the British Ministry of Information, necessary for that country's sense of identity. Nonetheless, her short stories of this period portray Ireland as an unreal, unchanging place cut off from what was happening in the rest of Europe.

'Sunday Afternoon', likely based on one of several information-gathering trips Bowen made back to Ireland during the war, draws a contrast between wartime London and neutral Ireland as Henry Roussel, who has lost all his possessions during the bombing of his London flat, briefly visits old friends in Ireland. Anglo-Irish and now elderly, their way of living has not been altered by the war and their lives have for Henry 'an air of being secluded behind glass' (*CS*: 616). They are horrified, in a Jamesian way, to hear of the loss of 'his beautiful things', but would prefer him not to enter into details about life during the Blitz. Their indifference to the war is portrayed as deplorable, yet Henry cannot help contrasting the graciousness of the Anglo-Irish way of life with the breakdown in language and identity experienced by those living through the Blitz in London when 'One's feelings seem to have no language for anything so preposterous' (*CS*: 617).

Only the young girl, Maria, is energized by Henry's description of life in wartime London. Maria, whom Henry, referencing *The*

Tempest, insists on calling Miranda, is eager to leave her enchanted island in order to participate in the war effort in London, ruthlessly dismissing the Ivy Compton-Burnett type dialogue of her elders who wish her to stay in Ireland. Though recognizing the paralysis of the Anglo-Irish, Henry refuses to aid Maria's getaway, telling her that the brave new world she envisages is one where the brutality of war has caused language, and even personal identity, to all but disappear. In contrast with the stylized civilities of the Anglo-Irish in neutral Ireland, life in London has been reduced to the mere will to survive: depersonalisation and the brute struggle for survival are all that await Maria, this world-weary Prospero warns. In London, she will have an identity number but no identity.

In 'Unwelcome Idea', the conflicted attitudes of the Irish to the war become apparent in the conversation on the tram between Miss Kevin and Mrs Kearney during which opinions range from that of Miss Kevin's father who displays ambivalent support for Hitler, to Mrs Kearney who sees the war chiefly as an obstacle to her social life (the Horse Show has been cancelled) and whose sister has scurried away to County Cavan in fright. Bowen satirises a country that does not know whether to treat the war as a major threat or a minor inconvenience. In 'A Love Story', the opening description of the mist's 'muffling silence' (*CS*: 497) conjures up a country where energy is paralysed, preparing us for the stifling relationship between Clifford Perry-Dunton, an Englishman stranded in Ireland since the outbreak of war, and his wife, Polly, who holds the purse strings and has no intention of letting him return to the dangers of wartime England.

'The Happy Autumn Fields' contrasts London during the Blitz with nineteenth-century Anglo-Ireland. Mary, inhabitant of a bombed out London house, whiles away the time between explosions by going through a series of letters the bomb blast has thrown up, much as Bowen herself had been reading through old family documents during the writing of *Bowen's Court*. The letters portray a Victorian Anglo-Irish family on an autumn day.

Ireland is not named in the story but Bowen later confirmed that the setting was County Cork (*LCW*: 61). Their solid personalities and intense passions seem more real to Mary than those of the desiccated inhabitants of wartime London where, she reflects:

> Everything pulverizes so easily because it is rot-dry ... the source, the sap must have dried up ... So much flowed through people; so little flows through us. All we can do is imitate love or sorrow (*CS*: 684).

Feeling that the dead are more alive than she is, Mary begins to dream about the lives of Henrietta and Sarah and their siblings. Yet, as always in Bowen, the Anglo-Irish world turns out to be less secure than it seems: Mary's anxiety in her bombed-out London home is mirrored in Anglo-Irish Henrietta's fear that she is about to lose her sister Sarah to her suitor, Eugene. The story suggests that Henrietta's hostility indirectly causes Eugene's uncanny death, thrown from his horse in the middle of empty fields, an instability foreshadowed in the opening scene when Emily, kneeling down to retie her boot lace, causes the line of Victorian children to topple over.

In 'Summer Night', wartime Ireland is the backdrop for an exploration of Bowen's characteristic themes of the breakdown of language and the fracturing of individual and political identities. The Irish countryside through which Emma speeds on the way to meet her lover is strangely insubstantial in the evening light and even the car in which she travels is unstable, lacking boundaries and open to the evening air. The instability, the sense of boundaries collapsing, even Emma's febrile impatience to be with her lover (Bowen described the Second World War as a time when, not knowing whether they would survive another day, people were more than usually promiscuous) are all themes common to Bowen's wartime writing, but there are elements in this story that more particularly reflect the Irish situation. Emma, for example, would seem deliberately drawn to represent traits Bowen thought characteristic of neutral Ireland. In 'Eire'[sic], Bowen commented that Ireland's neutrality and isolation from the war resulted in 'a national childishness, a lack of grasp on the general scheme of the world' (*MT*: 33). In her story Emma embodies this 'childishness', her bare legs and crumpled coat conveying an impression of a 'childish, blown little woman' (*CS*: 585), her excitement only possible in someone who, unlike her husband, the Major, has shut out all thoughts of the war. With her foolish romantic fantasy about a man as pragmatic and practised in love as Robinson, Emma displays that 'inhibition of judgement' Bowen feared would result from Irish neutrality (*MT*: 33).

In Vivie, the daughter who resembles her mother, Emma's uncivilized behaviour comes home to roost as Vivie's pre-pubertal sexuality manifests in a series of anarchical scenes associated by Aunt Fran with the outbreak of evil in the house. Emma's implied failure to inculcate moral standards in her children is a portent of the next generation's barbarism and she represents all that Bowen feared Ireland would become as a consequence of its policy of neutrality. The house itself is in a state of decay and there is a lack of communication between its inhabitants: Emma lies about her assignation with Robinson, the Major has few thoughts to spare from the war, while Aunt Fran complains that no one speaks the truth to her. The portrait of a house being destroyed by treachery from within foreshadows Robert Kelway's home in *The Heat of the Day*.

Other characters in the story embody attitudes Bowen thought characteristic of Ireland during the Emergency. Justin experiences that feeling of entrapment and stultification which Bowen saw as a particular threat to Ireland's intellectual life during the war, resulting from the suspension of travel between Ireland and Britain: 'We can no longer express ourselves: what we say doesn't even approximate to reality; it only approximates to what's been said', he complains (*CS*: 590). Justin's feeling that language is breaking down and must be renewed brings with it a concomitant, almost Beckettian, observation that personal identity is also dissolving and will need to be remade: 'On the far side of the nothing – my new form. Scrap "me"; scrap my wretched identity and you'll bring to the open some bud of life. I *not* "I"' (*CS*: 591). His perception that the war, even in neutral Ireland, is ushering in 'a new form for thinking and feeling' (*CS*: 589) is reinforced by his deaf sister, Queenie, who inhabits a silent, dreamy, 'underwater' world from which she occasionally emerges to make observations that while having 'no surface context, were never quite off the mark' and pose a challenge to Justin's linear patterns of thought (*CS*: 587).

In Bowen's stories war, even in neutral Ireland, reawakens trauma, ushers in obsessions, and reopens old wounds as her characters, torn from familiar surroundings, are forced to look deeper into life's abysses than they wish. Wartime brought her writing to new levels of excellence so that by now she was, as *The Irish Times* noted, 'accepted as a master of the short story form' (*The Irish Times* 5 January (1946): 4).

CHAPTER FIVE

Wartime Writing: *Bowen's Court* and *The Heat of the Day*

In *The Death of the Heart*, Matchett views the Quaynes' refusal to preserve memories and traditions, together with Anna's failure to produce an heir, as part of their 'mistaken approach to life': 'They'd rather no past – not have the past, that is to say. No wonder they don't rightly know what they're doing. Those without memories don't know what is what' (*DH*: 80). It was a similar consciousness of history having run out for her family that led Bowen, at a time when she was writing down her impressions of the Second World War – in her short stories, essays, reports for the British government, and the novel that was to become *The Heat of the Day* (1949) – to give, in *Bowen's Court* (1942), an imaginative reconstruction of the three hundred years of the Bowen family's residence in Ireland. During a period when, as a result of wartime confusions and dislocations, all identity seemed particularly fragile, Bowen turned to memory and her Anglo-Irish heritage to create a place of stability for herself (Breen, 2009: 115). In 'The Short Story in England' (1945), she commented:

> In wartime, the surface being itself uneasy, he [the writer] plumbs through to, and renders, unchanging and stable things – home feeling, human affection, old places, childhood memories (*PPT*: 314).

Bowen was not naïve about her undertaking; she was aware that historical memoirs were bound to be at least partly fictitious: 'As things are, the past is veiled from us by illusion – our own illusion. It is that which we seek. It is not the past but the idea of the past which draws us' (*MT*: 58). Basing her account on family papers, wills, letters, journals, law reports, oral family history, and published historical sources, and using invention to fill in lacunae, Bowen presents the Anglo-Irish as a courageous and glamorous race that came to full stature in the late eighteenth century with Grattan's Parliament and the Irish Volunteers, and continued to retain elements of prestige and status into the twentieth. Beneath the surface, however, her at once romantic and satirical family portrait projects a sense of unease, as if this bravura performance were about to be exposed at any moment. Even the opening lyrical passages describing the peace and stillness of the countryside around Bowen's Court are undercut by reminders of Edmund Spenser's unhappy stay in the neighbourhood and, a few pages later, by mention of the Desmond rebellions, the tense, violent final years of the British army garrison at Fermoy before independence, and the subsequent burning down of the barracks during the civil war. If her ancestors lacked insight into their ambivalent situation in Ireland Bowen, the last of the line, does not, acknowledging that the seeds of the Bowens' fall were there from the beginning: 'The Protestant newcomers' liveliness and well-being was wholly at the native Catholic expense' (*BC*: 129).

The fact that Bowen's Court, built by 1775, remained unfinished due to the debts that Henry Bowen III incurred during its construction was an ominous sign. In building his Big House, Henry Bowen might suggest the way he hoped future generations of Bowens would live, but he could foresee neither changes in politics, the personalities of his heirs, nor financial embarrassments, all of which ultimately, as Bowen's history shows, were to undermine Henry's original grand design for living. In her afterword for the second edition of 1964, by which time Bowen's

Court had been sold and demolished, Bowen admits that the image of Bowen's Court that she carried with her throughout the war was not quite the whole story:

> Yes, there was the picture of peace – in the house, in the country round. Like all pictures, it did not quite correspond with any reality. Or, you might have called the country a magic mirror, reflecting something that could not really exist. That illusion – peace at its most ecstatic – I held to, to sustain me throughout the war. I suppose everyone, fighting or just enduring, carried within him one private image, one peaceful scene. Mine was Bowen's Court (*BC*: 457).

Immediately she adds an undermining qualification: 'War made me that image out of a house built of anxious history' (*BC*: 457). As Neil Corcoran has argued, there is an alternative story of insanity, ghosts and Protestant Gothic fatality running beneath the narrative of the Bowen family, culminating in her father's breakdown (Corcoran, 2004: 26–31).

At the same time, though the world of Henry Bowen III might seem 'a Philistine, snobbish, limited and on the whole pretty graceless society' (*BC*: 125), Bowen wonders whether her own sophisticated, cosmopolitan world is any better:

> And to what did our fine feelings, our regard for the arts, our intimacies, our inspiring conversations, our wish to be clear of the bonds of sex and class and nationality, our wish to be fair to every one bring us? To 1939 (*BC*: 125).

In the context of western democracies convulsed by the Second World War, the world of Henry Bowen III, though built on more precarious foundations than he knew, had things in its favour: 'he got somewhere, and lived to die in his drawing-room surrounded by hosts of children and the esteem of what looked like a lasting order' (*BC*: 125). To Bowen, writing from the perspective of war-torn London where one was likely to be blown to pieces at any moment, this world had something to offer. In 'The Big House' (1940), she calls for modern day Ireland to find a way of accommodating its Big Houses and, by extension, the Anglo-Irish in the future life of the nation.

In the same year that *Bowen's Court* was published, Bowen also produced a short, personal memoir, *Seven Winters*, describing her childhood, with its rhythm of summers at Bowen's Court and winters in Dublin, in the years before her father's breakdown. The portrayal of an enclosed Irish Protestant world of weekday walks with her governess in certain carefully selected areas south of the Liffey, shopping in Upper Baggot Street, Sunday worship at St Stephen's, depicts a life seemingly built on secure foundations, but that safety too is revealed as ultimately illusory, blown apart by her father's nervous breakdown and the hurried removal of herself and her mother to England. At seven, Bowen had had her 'first comprehension of life as being other than mine' (*BC*: 52).

The focus on her family history and her early life in Ireland suggests the way in which the Second World War exacerbated Bowen's conflict over her hyphenated Anglo-Irish identity at a time when England was at war and Ireland remained neutral. Her 1941 essay, 'Eire'[sic], shows her attempting to hold the balance between the British view of Irish neutrality as 'a passively hostile and in some senses rather inhuman act' and Irish insistence that neutrality was 'Eire's first major independent act' and therefore of huge importance to that country's sense of identity (*MT*: 30–35).

Although she elected to stay in London for the duration of the war, working as an Air Raid Precautions warden patrolling the streets at night as Connie does in *The Heat of the Day* Bowen, perhaps naively, took the view that because of their hybrid identity, the Anglo-Irish had a duty to mediate between the English and the Irish. With this in mind, in response to the shattering blow of France's fall to the Germans – 'More loss had not seemed possible after that fall of France', thinks Stella in *The Heat of the Day* (*HD*: 94) – Bowen approached the Ministry of Information in London to inquire whether there was any work she could do in Ireland to help the war effort. She discussed this venture with Virginia Woolf in a letter dated 1 July 1940, but with none of her Irish friends. The Ministry of Information sent her to Ireland to gather information secretly on the political climate in Ireland among Dublin politicians and intellectuals, and among country people in County Cork. She was to test public opinion on the politically sensitive topic of England reclaiming the strategically important treaty ports for the duration of the war.

Between October 28 and November 6, 1940 Bowen, presenting herself as 'having a rest' from wartime London, occupied a flat overlooking Stephen's Green and held 'conversations' with interesting people 'over tea or sherry' (*SIW*: 55). Although an admirer of Churchill, in her report of 9 November 1940 Bowen warned that any attempt to repossess the treaty ports would be met by strenuous resistance from Ireland and would increase ill-feeling towards the English in a country that until then had been largely for the Allies. As in her published essay, she attempted to hold the balance between the two countries: 'The charge of "disloyalty" against the Irish has always, given the plain facts of history, irritated me. I could wish that the English kept history in mind more, that the Irish kept it in mind less' (*SIW*: 54). Somewhat paradoxically, given her wish to mediate between the two countries, her report was particularly severe on those Anglo-Irish who represented themselves as 'England's stronghold' in Ireland. She suggested that the Anglo-Irish would do better to merge their interests entirely with that of the new Ireland (*SIW*: 59). This report earned Bowen the commendation of Lord Cranborne, Head of the Dominions Office and he sent it to the Foreign Office for Lord Halifax's personal attention.

By 1942, Bowen's reports were less sympathetic towards Irish isolationism, painting a picture of a demoralised, depressed country subject to all the discomforts of wartime rationing and shortages as England but without the same underlying patriotic stimulus: '"The Emergency" is not a very inspiring flag around which to rally', she remarked drily in her report of 19 July 1942 (*SIW*: 88). After her death, when her role in supplying the Ministry of Information in London with reports was revealed, Bowen's behaviour was seen in some quarters as espionage and the revelation damaged her reputation, in Ireland particularly (*SIW*: 11–13).

While Bowen's wartime short stories were published in 1945, her novel took longer to appear. By 1944 she had written the first five chapters of *The Heat of the Day* and sent duplicates out of London for safekeeping (Glendinning, 1978: 187), but when she returned to the chapters at the end of the war she found her ideas had changed and the novel was not published until 1949.

The Heat of the Day opens, like *The Death of the Heart*, in Regent's Park, but in a park transformed by war with exhausted, shabby, dislocated Londoners drawn together on the first Sunday of September 1942 to listen to a concert: 'the music entered senses, nerves, and fancies that had been parched' (*HD*: 8). There are vivid descriptions in the novel of the atmosphere in London the morning after an air raid, of the privations of food rationing and of the difficulties of wartime travel, but *The Heat of the Day* is not primarily a realist novel. Like the stories in *The Demon Lover* (1945) which Bowen described as 'studies of climate, war-climate, and of the strange growths it raised' (*MT*: 95) *The Heat of the Day*, though seeming to employ some of the conventions of a spy thriller, is a tale of wartime espionage and betrayal that focuses on the effect of treachery on the private lives of individuals. It is wartime writing – and Bowen labelled all wartime writing resistance writing (*MT*: 97) – but it is not a story of action, 'the grind and scream of battles', but of indoor rooms where the action is plotted on foot of the kind of conversations Bowen was having in Ireland: 'this was a war of dry cerebration inside windowless walls' (*HD*: 142).

As Bowen sought to portray the ambivalences and uncertainties, the entangled loyalties and the sheer strangeness of life in wartime, her style became more knotted and evasive, her syntax with its double negatives, inversions, passive constructions, even more intense and jarring. In a 1950 radio broadcast, she compared the structure of *The Heat of the Day* to 'the convulsive shaking of a kaleidoscope, a kaleidoscope also of which the inside reflector was cracked' (*LI*: 283). In her discussion of *The Heat of the Day*, Anna Teekell argues that Bowen's tortuous sentences reflect a wartime atmosphere of suspicion and betrayal with double and even triple negatives 'encoding distrust into the syntax of the novel' and demanding constant vigilance from the reader in order to gather information (Teekell, 2011: 63). In *The Heat of the Day*, which many critics see as her finest novel, Bowen's style and subject matter found their perfect match, forging 'an altered style which, in its twists and syntactical strains, seems to enact the very pressure of aerial bombardment' (Coughlan, 2018: 219).

One aspect of Bowen's portrayal of the psychological impact of war on the inner lives of her characters is her understanding of the different ways people sought to resist its deadening impulse – through books (*MT*: 97), consoling dreams (*MT*: 96), alternative places of the imagination ('Mysterious Kôr'), and love affairs. In *The Heat of the Day* the romance between Stella Rodney and Robert Kelway begun during the Blitz, two years before the opening of the novel, is a form of resistance to the war. Occupied in 'secret, exacting, not unimportant war work' (*HD*: 26) for the Allies Stella, intelligent, articulate, well-connected and, like Bowen, approximately the same age as the century, constructs her affair with Kelway as a place of refuge in time of war: 'a hermetic world, which, like the ideal book about nothing, stayed itself on itself by its inner force' (*HD*: 90). There is an echo here of the description in *Bowen's Court* of the way in which the Bowens constructed their Big House, 'like Flaubert's ideal book about nothing' sustaining itself 'by the inner force of its style' (*BC*: 21). The description indicts both: Stella must learn what the Anglo-Irish learned too late, that the private world cannot be divorced from its political context. Her romance eventually turns out to have engaged her unknowingly on the enemy side. As a strategy for survival, Stella's hermetic love affair is impossible because it leaves out the 'third presence' of history, as is borne in on her when the original cataclysm in the novel, the war, is compounded by the invasion of her home by the undercover government agent, the lower-class Harrison, who spies on her elegant flat 'like a German in Paris' (*HD*: 44).

Harrison, for whom war has provided an unprecedented opportunity to develop his particular talents, informs Stella that Kelway, who works at the War Office, is suspected of passing secrets to the Germans. He offers to cover this up if Stella sleeps with him but warns her that if she tells Kelway he will know immediately: 'I've never yet known a man not change his behaviour once he's known he's watched' (*HD*: 37). Here the political invades the personal to a greater extent even than in *The Last September* as Harrison informs Stella that both she and her lover have been under surveillance for some time and not only by him. Stella realises that: '… they were not alone, nor had they been from the start, from the start of love. Their time sat in the third place at their table. They were the creatures of history' (*HD*: 194). In the atmosphere of paranoia and suspicion created by the war – 'Everywhere hung the heaviness of the even worse you could not be told and could not desire to hear' (*HD*: 92–3) – Stella is vulnerable to Harrison's suggestion that if Kelway is able to conceal his political treachery, he may also be capable of acting the lover, underlining the difficulty of knowing the truth, either in war or in love. '*If* actor, to her and for her so very good an actor, then why not actor also of love?' (*HD*: 173), she wonders, in a faint echo of Fanny Price's doubts about Henry Crawford in *Mansfield Park*.

In war, bombs obliterate personal and public landmarks, destabilising identity, which is further shattered by wartime displacements. When identity is fragile, people live in the moment, not knowing whether they will be alive the next day. In such circumstances people self-invent: 'Life-stories were shed as so much superfluous weight' (*HD*: 95). In the 'loose little society of the garrison' of people left behind in London strangers meet, like Stella and Kelway, in random bars or clubs and ask very little about one another's pasts (*HD*: 95). The claustrophobic psychological climate produced by living with daily fear of bombardment and death, wartime propaganda and surveillance, increases the difficulty of establishing the truth about anything: 'You did not know what you might not be tuning in to, you could not say what you might not be picking up: affected, infected you were at every turn' (*HD*: 248). For a counter spy like Harrison this is an opportunity: 'This is where I come in', he tells Stella (*HD*: 34).

To Stella, Harrison seems a scarcely believable character, constantly re-inventing himself:

> By the rules of fiction, with which life to be credible must comply, he was as a character 'impossible' – each time they met, for instance, he showed no shred or trace of having been continuous since they last met (*HD*: 140).

The prevalence of theatrical vocabulary in the novel around issues of identity increases the sense of instability. Stella's twenty-year-old son, Roderick, welcomes war as an opportunity to construct an adult identity but, when he visits his mother in her temporary furnished flat, for her sake he makes an awkward attempt to act his premilitary self: 'His body could at least copy, if not at once regain, unsoldierly looseness and spontaneity' (*HD*: 48). The peculiar doubling of names in the novel, Louie Lewis, Roderick Rodney, the ironically named Victor, Stella's ex-husband, who returns from the First World War, like Victor Ammering in *The Hotel*, a wounded and changed man, as well as the moments when Colonel Pole calls Roderick Robert by mistake, and Donovan misnames Harrison as Robertson, all suggest the fictitiousness and interchangeability of identity. Not knowing who or what to believe, anyone becomes capable of anything and so Harrison makes a reluctant spy of Stella who, after his revelations, starts to check up on Kelway.

Like *The House in Paris, The Heat of the Day* contains an Irish interlude when Stella travels to Ireland to inspect Mount Morris, the Irish estate where she spent her honeymoon with Victor, where her son Roderick was conceived and which he has unexpectedly inherited from his dead father's cousin, Francis Morris. Like Bowen herself, Roderick invests emotionally in his inheritance as a source of identity and continuity in the midst of war and is determined to preserve its traditions: 'The house, non-human, became the hub of his imaginary life' (*HD*: 50). Stella, whose family in the not too distant past were landed gentry, is more sceptical. Acknowledging that her generation is the missing link in the chain of the history of this house to the extent of feeling 'its broken edges' 'grating inside her soul' (*HD*: 176), an uncomfortable metaphor for her perception of her ambiguous status as divorcée and then widow, Stella recognises the attractions of Mount Morris as a stable repository of values and a refuge from the war. Conscious, however, of her own failure to fit into the expected narrative for upper-middle-class women, she has an instinctive sense of Mount Morris as a place of unhappiness for generations of Anglo-Irish women who, unable to break out of the already doomed pattern of Big House life, are reduced to exchanging silent, warning glances.

In *Bowen's Court* Bowen noted the scant attention paid to daughters and sisters in Bowen family history (*BC*: 77–8); in *The Heat of the Day* she produces an example in Cousin Francis' wife, Nettie. Driven to the point of madness, or feigned madness, by the expectations laid upon her as mistress of Mount Morris where she is expected to perpetuate the patriarchal traditions of the colonialist order by producing a male heir, Nettie has voluntarily left the family home for Wistaria Lodge, a private home for the mentally ill. Preferring this life in limbo, in a Hamlet-like feigning of insanity, to forced participation in the Ascendancy narrative of wife and mother, Nettie's happiest days are when she forgets she ever had a husband and a home. In one way, Nettie's escape is enabling, freeing her from the Big House narrative for her life. 'Here I am and you can't make any more stories out of that', she tells Roderick (*HD*: 214). In another, it underlines Nettie's powerlessness: her retreat from one sort of imposed silence into a silence more freely chosen is silence nonetheless in a life isolated from political realities.

Roderick is all the more convinced that his destiny is Mount Morris since, standing 'geographically' outside the war it will, he believes, be better able to avoid the cataclysms brought about by that event. However the picture Bowen paints of wartime Ireland, drawing on her trips back to Ireland for the British Ministry of Information, is full of ambivalences. Despite wartime propaganda, eagerly repeated by Kelway's sister, Ernestine, neutral Ireland also suffers from shortages. Nor is it entirely cut off from the war: if wartime Ireland was a refuge, it was also a place of treachery where infiltration by spies for both sides was a problem (Wills, 2007: 147). At Mount Morris, Stella learns that Harrison has visited the estate, probably to try to recruit Cousin Francis as a spy for the British in Ireland. Bowen's portrayal of Cousin Francis reveals the divided loyalties of the Anglo-Irish: ashamed of Ireland's neutrality he offers his services to the British War Office, but when his boyhood friend, Colonel Pole, makes a snide remark about Irish neutrality, he fires back a stiff letter 'fairly blowing my head off – this and that and the other in a pretty nearly nationalistic strain' (*HD:* 81). When Francis' loyal retainer, Donovan, triumphantly announces Montgomery's victory at El Alamein, his daughter, Hannah, receives the news 'indifferent as a wand' (*HD*: 178), suggesting Irish disaffection from events so crucial for the English and by extension for their colonial allies, the Anglo-Irish. Even with her greater wartime nostalgia for the Big House, Bowen cannot quite conceal from herself tensions between the Anglo-Irish and their Irish neighbours.

As in *The House in Paris*, the stay in Ireland proves a turning point, both politically (the news of Allied victories in North Africa) and in Stella's personal life as she receives from Donovan proof that Harrison was telling the truth about his visits to Mount Morris and therefore may well be telling the truth about everything else. She returns from Ireland determined to interrogate Kelway and, as a first move, accompanies him to his family home, Holme Dene.

The Heat of the Day extends Bowen's satire on the insular and complacent English middle classes as the suburban English home in wartime becomes a site of treachery and paranoia. Given that a proportion of Irish people favoured the German side during the war, Kelway's allegiance to a Nietzschean fascism has been read as an Irish trace (McCormack, 1993: 232–40). The fact that treachery is located in the heart of an *English* family shows how deeply divided Bowen's own loyalties were during the war, deeper than she may ever have acknowledged. In Ireland, where she would have met people sympathetic, however discreetly, to the Germans, she noted a fascist element in Irish political debate; in England, where she encountered hostility towards Irish neutrality shading in people's minds into Irish treachery, she complained of anti-Irish prejudice.

In Holme Dene, the Kelways' crypto-fascist house where, like any psychologist, Stella goes back to Kelway's childhood roots to uncover the reasons for his treachery, his 'case-history' (*HD*: 103), she finds a house to breed a traitor, an inauthentic building, with alcoves and inglenooks and 'swastika-arms of passage leading to nothing' (*HD*: 258), its corridors full of 'repressions, doubts, fears, subterfuges, and fibs' (*HD*: 256). Watched over by Mrs Kelway, strategically knitting in the centre of the lounge from which panopticon she can oversee every movement in the house, this is a home where the occupants, like spies, can never afford to be off their guard:

Their private hours, it could be taken, were spent in nerving themselves for inevitable family confrontations such as meal-times, and in working on to their faces the required expression of having nothing to hide (*HD*: 256).

Like his *doppelgänger* Harrison, Robert Kelway is rootless: in London, he stays at Stella's flat but has other 'haunts', and the stability of his apparently quintessential Home Counties home is undermined by being permanently for sale. Before that, he tells Stella, the Kelways moved several times between houses, shuffling their furniture around like so much stage scenery. 'How unsettling', Stella remarks (*HD*: 121). In her afterword to *Bowen's Court*, reflecting on the extent to which her portrait of the Bowen family was influenced by the wartime context, Bowen comments that, while the war may have led her to exaggerate the Bowens' propensity to dangerous fantasies, she was able to show that landed property protected her ancestors from the worst excesses of the will to power:

> For these people – my family and their associates – the idea of power was mostly vested in property (property having been acquired by use or misuse of power in the first place). One may say that while property lasted the dangerous power-idea stayed, like a sword in its scabbard, fairly at rest (*BC*: 455).

Whatever the Bowens' Catholic tenants and neighbours down the centuries would have thought of the description of her ancestors' 'power-idea' remaining unused, the passage serves to highlight the vacuum in which Kelway's unrestrained will to power operates: 'the power-loving temperament is more dangerous when it either prefers or is forced to operate in what is materially a void. We have everything to dread from the dispossessed' (*BC*: 455).

Mrs Kelway, nicknamed Muttikins by her children, is in a line of manipulative older women in Bowen's work. Observing her successful reliance on gender stereotypes to control all aspects of life at Holme Dene, Stella pronounces her 'wicked' (*HD*: 110). Stella is struck by the ultra-femininity of Robert's mother, her petite frame, 'the miniature daunting beauty of that face', 'the relentlessly delicate' features (*HD*: 109). Ultra-feminine mothers are a feature of interwar women's writing, and are often portrayed as deeply damaging to daughters see, for example, May Sinclair's *The Life and Death of Harriett Frean* (1922), Radclyffe Hall's *The Unlit Lamp* (1924), and Winifred Holtby's *The Crowded Street* (1924). In Bowen's novel, it is the men of the family who suffer most. In Holme Dene, this 'man-eating house' (*HD*: 257), silence, broken only by coruscating remarks, is the method by which Muttikins imposes a patriarchal standard of heroic male behaviour on her husband and her son, both of whom in different ways fail to live up to her masculine ideal: 'Mrs Kelway's way of saying "your father" still, years after that guilty creature's death, vibrated with injury; the implication was that he had become a father at her expense' (*HD*: 257). Mrs Kelway's feminine tyranny reduces Robert and his father to silence. In her presence, Robert explains to Stella, they had difficulty meeting one another's gaze:

'We were an attractive embarrassment to each other – and, of course, in this house we were thrown very much together. Something was expected: very often I did not know which way to look and looking back I can see that he didn't either' (*HD*: 118–19).

War, in particular, is a masculine activity and Muttikins turns the retreat of Dunkirk into Robert's personal failure: 'Mrs Kelway, whose distant ice-clear gaze had not left her son's face since his last remark, said: "But retreats are now a thing of the past"' (*HD*: 114). In an effort to impress on Robert what is expected of him his mother and sister have hung up photographs of himself from every stage of his life. Robert refers to this as his 'criminal record', testifying to the mendacious performance of boyhood and masculinity he believes he has been forced into ever since he was born. He asks Stella: 'Can you think of a better way of sending a person mad than nailing that pack of his own lies all round the room where he has to sleep?' (*HD*: 118).

In reaction against his impotent, emotionally castrated father and the claustrophobic feminine world created by his mother at Holme Dene Robert, psychically wounded by his upbringing and physically wounded at Dunkirk, embraces the ultra-masculine world of the Nietzschean *Übermensch*, seeing in fascism the glorification of the masculinity that both he and his father have failed to achieve: 'It bred my father out of me, gave me a new heredity', he explains to Stella (*HD*: 273). 'Who could want to be free when he could be strong?' (*HD*: 269). This war, he tells Stella, is different from the one in which her brothers were killed. The retreat from Dunkirk has caused Kelway to lose faith in his country and in patriotism as a concept, and he betrays his country less out of positive conviction than from despair at his loss of belief in words like honour, patriotism, loyalty and democracy. In her review of Angus Calder's *The People's War* (1969), a book that exposes truths untold by wartime propaganda, Bowen reveals herself to have been aware, even at the time, of the difference between public propaganda around Dunkirk and her own experience of 'disaffection, a raw black bitterness in the disarmed army back from Dunkirk ... on a scale not to be measured then' (*MT*: 182). Stella notices that Robert's limp varies according to his mood: 'The variation, she had discovered, had like that in a stammer a psychic cause – it was a matter of whether he did or did not, that day, feel like a wounded man' (*HD*: 90).

The pressures of war give added urgency in *The Heat of the Day* to Bowen's characteristic themes of dislocation and the fragility of identity. In the final scene between Stella and her lover, identity becomes so unstable that spy and counter-spy,

Kelway and Harrison, who share the same first name, appear interchangeable to Stella: 'It seemed to her it was Robert who had been the Harrison' (*HD*: 275). Kelway, whose unequal gait finds its match in Harrison's 'uneven eyes' (*HD*: 29), has been the one who has viewed everything – newspaper headlines, rumours, radio announcements – from the point of view of a spy. Notwithstanding her love for him, Stella in the end resists Kelway's nihilistic despair, insisting that words still carry meaning. '"No, but you cannot say there is not a country!" she cried aloud, starting up. She had trodden every inch of a country with him ...' (*HD*: 274). Despite her own lack of a permanent home Stella finally chooses, over Kelway's abstractions, that private attachment to place which resists the depersonalisations of war and justifies for her, as for her brothers, fighting in defence of one's country.

One of the weapons Mrs Kelway employs to establish her power is a withholding silence, as if words belong to the male order of things from which she, as a woman, is exempt: 'For, why *should* she speak? She had all she needed: the self-contained mystery of herself. Her lack of wish for communication showed in her contemptuous use of words' (*HD*: 108–9). Outside the gates of her own home, however, Muttikins' power stops, like that of Hannah Kernahan in Kate O'Brien's *The Last of Summer* (1943), with whom she shares some features. Female powerlessness is the price to be paid for colluding with patriarchal gender roles. If in *The Death of the Heart*, Portia has to leave behind wordless communication with her mother in order to enter the grown-up world of language and civilisation, in *The Heat of the Day* adult women like Nettie and Stella are silenced. At the inquest, where the causes of Kelway's death prove inconclusive but where Stella's private sexual behaviour is put on trial, even the articulate Stella is unable to challenge people's misreading of her as a *femme fatale*, recalling the earlier time when she was unable to shake people's conviction that she was the guilty party in her divorce from Victor.

Problems with language are a particular concern for Louie

Lewis, a young factory worker stranded in wartime London by the bomb that killed her parents and flattened her home in Seale-on-Sea (Hythe again). Missing her husband Tom, overseas in the army, Louie, like the orphaned Portia in *The Death of the Heart*, is waiting for someone to give her a clue as to how to live her life: 'she looked about her in vain for someone to imitate; she was ready, nay eager to attach herself to anyone who could seem to be following any one course with certainty' (*HD*: 15). Louie lacks the words to describe her predicament until wartime propaganda in the newspapers supplies her with a series of identities: 'Was she not a worker, a soldier's lonely wife, a war orphan, a pedestrian, a Londoner, a home-and animal-lover, a thinking democrat, a movie-goer, a woman of Britain, a letter writer, a fuel-saver, and a housewife?' (*HD*: 152). Later, Louie finds another role model in Stella whom she admires because Stella uses language beautifully and seems 'too good for the world' (*HD*: 306). This lasts until, at the inquest, Stella is portrayed in the newspapers by which Louie sets such store, as a promiscuous woman given to drink and to entertaining men friends in her West End flat. The feeling that 'there was nobody to admire' (*HD*: 307) gives Louie permission to return to her old ways, adhering to her personal belief that 'she felt nearer Tom with any man than she did with no man' (*HD*: 145). Unfaithfulness becomes a kind of faithfulness and in 1944 it leads Louie to pregnancy, motherhood and further self-authoring: with Tom dead, Louie seizes the chance to be 'an orderly mother' (*HD*: 329). She returns to Seale-on-Sea with her son named Thomas Victor in a doubling of identities that ironises her desire to provide her son with the patriarchal father figure he so clearly lacks.

The conclusion of *The Heat of the Day* has been much debated, with some critics more optimistic than others about the future as embodied in the two main representatives of the younger generation, Louie and Roderick. Louie's 'now complete life' (*HD*: 329) as mother of Tom's child may, however misleadingly, be a hopeful sign for the future, the three Yeatsian swans flying west at the end of the novel, recalling the swans seen by Stella at Mount Morris and portending the direction where Bowen believed her own future lay, out of post-war socialist Britain, in Ireland. Nevertheless, in view of the tragedies that ensue in Bowen's work from adults making mysteries for children to grow up in, this script may be a false start for Louie's child who is likely to become as confused about his identity as Leopold in *The House in Paris*. Louie's willing abandonment of her factory work for motherhood underlines the fact that the increased number of women in the workplace – Louie's fellow lodger, Connie, is like Bowen, an ARP warden, while Ernestine belongs to the WVS – was only a temporary phenomenon. After the war women would be encouraged back into their traditional roles in the home (Plain, 1996: 28–9). Moreover, while the war was seen by many as an opportunity for greater mingling between the classes, those opportunities were often brief: Stella meets Louie in a bar. The disparity between Louie's monotonous factory work and Stella's interesting intelligence job underlines the fact that, notwithstanding rhetoric around the People's War, class hierarchies were temporarily disrupted but not permanently altered as a result of the war (Miller, 2010: 15–16).

Despite misgivings about Roderick's inheritance, Stella – like Bowen in 'The Big House' – pictures Mount Morris adapted to fit a modern age and Roderick farming his estate with the help of the local community: 'he had been fitted into a destiny; better, it seemed to her, than freedom in nothing' (*HD*: 175). She envisages him marrying a local Catholic girl, perhaps even Donovan's younger daughter, who would rearrange the furniture and stop him dwelling on past disasters by removing the picture of the *Titanic* in the drawing room. For Bowen, whose uncle went down on the ship, the sinking of the *Titanic* in 1912 'was the first black crack across the surface of *exterior* things' (*BC*: 423), marking the end of the pre-First World War world with its traditional loyalties. To jettison this picture reveals the extent to which Stella envisages a clean break with the past. Roderick himself is full of ideas for going to agricultural college and learning to farm the estate along modern scientific lines. However, Donovan's words, 'That way, you could sink a terrible lot of money' (*HD*: 313), and his memories of Cousin Francis's fanciful schemes for improvement, hint at the future doom of this project. Roderick's immaturity is further underlined when Donovan, whose perceptiveness, both about Mount Morris and about the conduct of the war, outstrips that of other characters, remarks that he has failed to protect Stella by insisting she remain safely in Ireland. If Roderick is to take on the role of Anglo-Irish patriarch, Donovan implies, he will have to do better than this.

Critics are divided too on whether the ending leaves Stella empowered (Lassner, 1990: 138–9) or representing the postwar containment of women (Plain, 1996: 185–7). During the renewed German attacks on London in February 1944, described by Mollie Panter-Downes in her *London War-Notes* as 'nastier, in a way, because they are more concentrated' (Panter-Downes, 2014: 380), Harrison returns. Kelway was probably right in believing that his reason for finally turning down Stella's offer to sleep with him was not because his feelings were hurt, but because some other job had come up. In wartime the personal counts for less than Stella thinks, and Harrison admits he had less power over the situation than he allowed her to believe: 'I was switched', he tells her (*HD*: 317). For Bowen, who had herself married an ex-soldier, Stella's prospective marriage to a brigadier, 'a cousin of a cousin' (*HD*: 321), might have signified a welcome return to order, though Bowen allows the marriage to remain as yet unachieved: 'prospects have alternatives … I always have left things open', Stella tells a disapproving Harrison (*HD*: 322). After Stella's wartime probing of conventions the reader cannot help but feel that for a woman who has twice sacrificed her good name to protect a man's reputation, such a marriage is a betrayal of her potential for change and a renunciation of her own happiness in favour of securing Roderick's position: the master of Mount Morris cannot 'go on and on having a disreputable mother', she tells Kelway (*HD*: 196).

It is part of the point of *The Heat of the Day*'s portrayal of the wartime atmosphere that mysteries remain unresolved. We never find out about the extent of the damage Kelway's betrayal did to his country. Nor do we discover Harrison's precise role in the war, though his after-life seems briefly delineated in the shadowy figure of the 'obsessed-looking' but now 'aimless' man who continues, a week after VE day, to haunt London's parks in 'I Hear You Say So', looking over his shoulder, surveying the crowds, old spy habits remaining though his occupation has gone (*CS*: 753). The novel's unanswered questions reflect the fact that knowledge in wartime is diffuse, and that to live through war is to have 'the sense of being narrated, of being part of a discourse you cannot control' (Corcoran, 2004: 171). In 1945 Bowen wrote: 'What was happening was out of all proportion to our faculties for knowing, thinking and checking up' (*MT*: 96). Her views did not change. In 1969 she commented

> The majority of us, living through those years, did not attempt to rationalize them, nor have most of us done so since. War is a prolonged passionate act, and we were involved in it. We at least knew that we only half knew what we were doing (*MT*: 182).

Aspects of Bowen's private life fed into *The Heat of the Day*. Foremost was her relationship with the novel's dedicatee, Charles Ritchie, another colonial outsider in London. Ritchie was sceptical in 1941 as to Britain's capacity to defeat Hitler and, as his diary reveals, almost from their first meeting he was unfaithful to her. Her friendship with Goronwy Rees, that disloyal lover who was a friend of Guy Burgess and therefore on the fringes of the Cambridge spy set that was to be unmasked in the 1950s, provided another element (Lee, 1999: 169–170). Bowen's own guilt and anxieties about her spying activities in Ireland found their way into the portrayal of Harrison and Kelway, their shared first name, Robert, being the name that she would have received had she been male. Her stammer has its counterpart in their disabilities (eye trouble, limp). *The Heat of the Day* might be described as the most subtly Irish of all of Bowen's novels, a novel about a British war that could only have been written by, in O'Faoláin's memorable phrase, a 'heart-cloven and split-minded' Anglo-Irish woman, convinced both of the need for attachment and the inevitability of not belonging (O'Faoláin, 1982: 15).

CHAPTER SIX

Time and Trauma: *A World of Love, The Little Girls,* and *Eva Trout, or Changing Scenes*

A World of Love (1955)

Early in 1952 Bowen, eager to quit an England that, under Attlee's Labour government, was changing in ways she did not welcome, moved back to Ireland intending to make her permanent home in Bowen's Court with Alan. The latter's sudden death in August 1952 left Bowen with sole responsibility for running her family estate. Determined to keep it as a refuge for herself and Ritchie, she immersed herself in journalism, broadcasting, and lecturing in American universities in order to pay for the upkeep. It is against this background that *A World of Love*, a work of mourning, loss and the effects of time, was written.

A World of Love returns to the Anglo-Irish setting of *The Last September* and a young girl on the brink of adulthood. Twenty-year-old Jane's first appearance in a trailing muslin dress found in the attic at Montefort makes her seem, in the 1950s, like a ghost from the Edwardian past, 'a Vision', as Kathie, the maidservant, declares (*WL*: 20). Jane's discovery, also in the attic, of Guy's letters written to an unknown addressee before his departure for the First World War, precipitates the cataclysm that will change all their lives by making him seem to live again. Picking up on

Bowen's ghost stories, notably 'The Demon Lover', *A World of Love* is a story of a prolonged haunting by Guy, killed fighting in France, as well as a meditation on the fictitiousness of memory (all the characters have their own version of Guy) and, since it is through his letters that Jane falls in love with Guy, a reminder of the power of writing. It is also Bowen's final fictional portrayal of the Big House and her farewell to a particular style of lyrical, elegiac writing.

By the 1950s most Irish Big Houses were in various stages of dilapidation, only a few managing to maintain pre-Second World War standards (Bence-Jones, 1987: 273–87). Montefort, a decaying 'small mansion', possesses merely 'a ghost' of style (*WL*: 9), its rutted tracks and closed front door marking the end of the Anglo-Irish hospitality that was once the *raison d'être* of such dwellings. At this stage of Montefort's life, the work of the farm takes precedence since it is agriculture, together with Antonia's earnings in London, which is keeping the house and its inhabitants afloat. Fred barely has time to spare from his work on the farm, while Lilia, his wife, is too shy even to attend church or to play the role of Anglo-Irish lady at the sole social event on Montefort's calendar, the Hunt Fête. Surrounded by felled trees, a further sign of economic necessity, the Big House has become 'a *bois dormant*' (*MT*: 25), a ghostly, barely visible, presence lingering in an indifferent Ireland. 'No idea anyone was living there', a local remarks (*WL*: 30).

This fairy tale atmosphere of a Sleeping Beauty place is also, as Clair Wills argues, linked to a specific social and political context, namely 1950s anxieties over mass emigration and the depopulation of the Irish countryside (Wills, 2009: 133–49). For the Anglo-Irish are not alone: the rest of Ireland is also struggling with poverty, emigration, and the failure of small farms, as is evident when Lilia and her daughters go on a shopping expedition to the neighbouring sleepy town of Clonmore. In 'Ireland Today', Bowen argued that neutrality had kept Ireland under wraps for six years, out of step with the modern world, and that the country was still, in the 1950s, trying to catch up (*SIW*: 170–82). 'To travel in Ireland', she wrote in a 1954 article for *Vogue*, 'is to travel some way back in time' (*SIW*: 182).

There are particular reasons why time at Montefort has stood still. *A World of Love*'s Beckettian opening sentence, incorporating the title of Bowen's previous novel, 'The sun rose on a landscape still pale with the heat of the day before' (*WL*: 9), indicates lives lived in the aftermath of two world wars. This is borne out by the reflection of Antonia, Guy's cousin, sometime lover, and inheritor of Montefort, that:

> These years she went on living belonged to him [Guy], his lease upon them not having run out yet. The living were living his lifetime; and of this his contemporaries – herself, Lilia, Fred – never were unaware. They were incomplete (*WL*: 45).

A 'studio portrait' of Guy in uniform hangs in the hall, reminding the inhabitants of present day Montefort of the dashing, stylish, aristocratic Anglo-Ireland of the past in whose shadow they all live, in the same way as the obelisk, monument to some forgotten Anglo-Irish ancestor, casts its long shadow over the house's decaying facade. The sense of lives suspended since Guy's death, evidenced by the stopped clock and out of date calendars in the kitchen, and the lack of electricity, plumbing, telephone and other modern conveniences, is intensified by the oppressive, disorientating heat that causes all of the characters to droop and wilt.

A World of Love may be glossed with Bowen's 1951 broadcast, 'The Cult of Nostalgia', and her essay 'The Bend Back' (written in 1951) where she warns writers of the dangers, after two world wars, of pandering to the general wish to look back to safer times. The First World War was a watershed: 'confidence was broken by 1914; from then on, decline of love for the present went with loss of faith in it' but, she asks, 'Why cannot the confidence in living, the engagement with living, the prepossession with living be re-won?' (*MT*: 54–5). Our view of the past, she argues, is always edited, falsified into 'heroic simplification'. The message of *A World of Love* is that the inhabitants of Montefort must avoid being trapped into mythologizing Anglo-Irish traditions.

The past, however, is not easily done away with, for Guy's death has locked Antonia, Lilia and Fred into a state of uneasy interdependence, akin to Cold War paralysis. Antonia, in her fifties like Bowen herself, spends half her time living and working in London and has won some acclaim as a photographer. Her attitude to Montefort, which her money helps to finance, is similar to that of Bowen towards Bowen's Court: 'Her overweening sentiment for the place went ... with neither wish nor ability to remain here always' (*WL*: 14). Antonia has taken over responsibility for Fred and Lilia's daughter, Jane, sending her to boarding school and to secretarial college in London, apparently grooming her to be the Montefort heir. At times, Antonia seems to think of Jane as her own child by Guy for it is Antonia who, some years after Guy's death, arranged the marriage between his former fiancée, Lilia, and Fred, illegitimate son of a Montefort uncle. Fred farms the land but is a pale substitute for Guy being regarded by his Anglo-Irish neighbours as of ambivalent status, neither gentry nor tenant, with a touch of 'foreign blood' (*WL*: 15). Now in her fifties, Lilia, 'half the hostess at Montefort, half not' (*WL*: 13), would be happier in the suburban home of her childhood rather than in 'this old terrible house' (*WL*: 13) where things never run smoothly. Her atavistic fears of Montefort being invaded by hostile outsiders, of the house going up in flames, and of being 'besieged, under observation or in some way even under a threat' (*WL*: 52), suggest a replaying of old Anglo-Irish traumas.

Up in the attics, Jane too feels burdened by Anglo-Irish history: 'the wreckage left by the past oppressed her – so much had been stacked up and left to rot; everything was derelict, done for, done with' (*WL*: 27). Her consciousness of 'this continuous tedious business of received grievances, not-to-be-settled old scores' (*WL*: 35) applies not only to the bickering and undercurrents between Fred, Lilia and Antonia, but to Ireland in the bitter aftermath of the civil war and the Emergency:

> The passions and politics of her family so much resembled those of the outside world that she made little distinction between the two. It was her hope that this might all die down, from lack of recruits or fuel or, most of all, if more people were to take less notice. She did what she could by adding no further heat … Most of all she mistrusted the past's activity and its queeringness – she knew no one, apart from her own contemporaries, who did not speak of it either with falsifying piety or with bitterness (*WL*: 34–5).

In 'The Cult of Nostalgia', Bowen notes that 'it is in the younger people that revulsion against nostalgia is most marked' (*LI*: 101). However in a novel whose theme is 'the disruptive return of the misunderstood, unprocessed past' (Pearson, 2015: 82), Jane has first to face the past in order to set it to rest before she can move forward into her future.

Jane's discovery of the letters stirs in all of them an awareness of 'the annihilating need left behind by Guy' (*WL*: 76). Imagining the letters are addressed to herself, Jane concocts a romance around them, Antonia is so unsettled she drives off alone to the sea, and Lilia has to lie down. The letters intensify Fred's consciousness that he is merely a substitute Guy and provoke twelve-year-old Maud's wrath that the letters are undermining her father's rightful status. Maud's physical scuffles with her familiar, Gay David, a demonic hangover from Anglo-Ireland's heyday, mirror the older generation's psychological struggles to overcome the effects of the past. As the letters circulate between Jane, Maud, Fred, Lilia, Antonia, Kathie and finally back to Jane again who burns them, the discovery that they are addressed, not to Antonia or Lilia, but to a third woman whose name Kathie eventually deciphers, breaks the spell for Lilia, whose identity, like that of many women after the First World War, has been bound up in being Guy's beloved: 'What had now happened must either kill her or, still worse, force her to live' (*WL*: 50). Lilia begins to assert her independence from Antonia by having her hair cut, by forging, in Clonmore, stronger bonds with Jane, and by re-opening a conversation with Fred, an 'act of love' (*WL*: 105) that acknowledges his importance in her life after years of estrangement.

As time and the outside world break into Montefort in the guise of Big Ben's chimes booming through the wireless, the bond between Antonia and Jane is broken. Perceiving that Antonia has aged, Jane acknowledges the inevitable supplanting of the generations and her own move forward into a separate future, while Antonia makes amends for her callous treatment of Lilia down the years with her compassionate lie that Guy's letters were indeed addressed to her. The lordly Anglo-Irish past turns out to be not so heroic after all. Guy has retained his hold over them through his absence; had he survived the war, the illusion would surely have been shattered since, a less than faithful lover, 'he had scattered round him more promises … than one man could have hoped to honour' (*WL*: 97). Similarly the obelisk, Antonia informs them at the end, in an echo of Somerville and Ross, was erected by a decidedly degenerate Anglo-Irish ancestor who married his cook and 'went queer in the head from drinking and thinking about himself' (*WL*: 137). If the inhabitants of Montefort are to move forward, not only Guy as a lover, but the entire burden of Anglo-Irish history once described by Bowen as 'the indefinite ghosts of the past' (*MT*: 28), has to be exorcised.

A World of Love is, among other things, an extended ghost story that suggests the First World War, in which so many heirs to Anglo-Irish estates lost their lives, has remained unfinished business:

> Something has challenged the law of nature: it is hard, for instance, to see a young death in battle as in any way the fruition of a destiny, hard not to sense the continuation of the apparently cut-off life, hard not to ask, but *was* dissolution possible so abruptly, unmeaningly and soon? And if not dissolution, instead, what? (*WL*: 44).

The novel explores that question through supernatural touches which, as in Sheridan Le Fanu's fiction, skilfully mingle the Gothic with the psychologically plausible. At Lady Latterly's séance-like dinner party Jane feels Guy present only after she has drunk three martinis, while Lilia's sense of Guy's presence in the walled garden is attributed by Fred to sunstroke on her newly bare neck. Unusually for Bowen, *A World of Love* invokes Irish legend in the guise of the *sidhe*, those fairy folk, both sinister and seductive, who charm young men and women into the realms of the dead and are especially dangerous for Jane on whom Guy's letters work like a spell (Tracy, 1998: 242–55).

Jane acts as a kind of medium for Guy, reflecting the fact that in the mid-twentieth-century vogue for spiritualism, mediums were sometimes associated with the teenage girl and her dangerously nascent sexuality (Hazelgrove, 2000: 172–92). In Bowen's novel though, despite the Gothic touches, Guy comes back, not to haunt his relatives, but as an act of love that releases them from their enslavement to the past and enables them to move forward: 'He came back, through Jane, to be let go', thinks Antonia. 'It was high time. When that clock struck, it said: "Enough!"' (*WL*: 135). This exorcism of the past is as necessary for Antonia, Lilia and Fred as it was for Bowen who, after her prolonged immersion in the world of her ancestors in *Bowen's Court*, wrote in the afterword: 'We cannot afford to have ghosts ... I wish not to drag up the past but to help lay it' (*BC*: 453). Guy's loving renunciation of claims on them contrasts with Maud's Old Testament curses, her judgemental attitudes a parodic example of the Bowen child whose part witting, part unwitting, candour cruelly exposes ethical flaws in the lives of the adults around her.

By the end of the novel Guy's act of love has worked, the Sleeping Beauty spell is broken, and Jane travels west, not to the Irish Revival's peasants and fishermen, but to modernity in the shape of Shannon airport, described by Bowen in 'A New Ireland 1950s' as 'that glaring no-place of runways, hut buildings, transatlantic airliners refuelling' (*SIW*: 159), where the Irish language has established precedence over English in public announcements and where awaits the American, Richard Priam, whose money may be the saving of Montefort. The ending of *A World of Love* indicates the modernity that Bowen, in 'Ireland, June 1954', insists underlies the appearance of a country seemingly in hock to the past: 'beneath the spell of monotony, Ireland *does* progress' (*SIW*: 182).

In this modern Ireland, even if political power and status have long since vanished, the Big House does still, Bowen argues, have a contribution to make: 'I believe it is possible to bring these beautiful legacies of the old world into line with the more arduous ideals of the new' (*SIW*: 131). Bowen is not here thinking of *nouveaux riches* like Lady Latterly, wealthy refugees from socialist Britain, often with no Irish ties, who were buying up large houses in Ireland and importing luxury and sophistication without fulfilling the kind of responsibilities to neighbours and tenants understood by the older gentry. By turning Montefort into a working farm, Fred, a hard taskmaster but respected by the locals if not by the gentry, has been able to adapt the house to the times in ways that do not damage the local community. The belligerence of his younger daughter, Maud, suggests that the spirit of the Protestant Ascendancy has not quite been vanquished.

At Shannon airport Jane, 'her trial lesson in love' (*WL*: 51) behind her, falls instantly in love with Richard Priam, as he does with her. *A World of Love* ends on a note of confidence in the future all the more remarkable in that the final chapters were written during a period of emotional turmoil for Bowen after Alan's death which had, by unbalancing the equality that had hitherto existed between Ritchie and herself, heightened her anguish over his marriage to Sylvia (*LCW*: 198–9). Ritchie interpreted the novel as portraying their 'shared illusion of life', a reference not only to their mutual faith in love, but also to their dream of one day living together at Bowen's Court (*LCW*: 199). However, though Ritchie took for himself *A World of Love*'s faith in love, this novel of 'mourning and living on' (Bennett and Royle, 1995: 113) may also be read as a lament for Alan, a decorated First World War soldier whose death left Bowen astray in ways even Ritchie failed to understand and of which we do not have the full record, since he destroyed her letters from this period (*LCW*: 185). In a letter to William Plomer dated May 1958, Bowen wrote: 'Alan never seems dead, in the sense that he never seems gone: I suppose that if one has lived the greater part of one's life with a person he continues to accompany one through every moment' (*MT*: 209). These sentiments, which perhaps she could not share with Ritchie, raise the question, underlined by the prefatory quote from the seventeenth-century mystic, poet, and theologian, Thomas Traherne, as to what kind of love Bowen is talking about in *A World of Love*.

Traherne, best-known for his *Centuries of Meditation* published in 1908 after their rediscovery in manuscript some ten years earlier, celebrates an almost childlike love of God, happiness, and delight in the natural world, themes that deeply influenced Bowen's friend, Iris Murdoch, and which have some bearing on Bowen's novel. The question of spiritual themes in modernist writing has been explored by scholars such as Maren Tova Linett (2007), Pericles Lewis (2010), Lara Vetter (2010), Suzanne Hobson (2011), Erik Tonning (2014), and Jane de Gay (2018). The question is particularly pertinent in Bowen's case since she was a regular churchgoer and in a letter to Ritchie, specifically mentions the Bible as an influence on *A World of Love*: 'I now can't read anything that isn't in some way relevant to that novel. I keep dashing to the Bible, for instance' (*LCW*: 173). Bowen was also at this time reading Arthur Eddington's immensely popular *The Nature of the Physical World* (1928) (*LCW*: 173) in the final chapters of which, after discussing the science behind quantum physics and theories of relativity, Eddington, an astronomer and physicist but also a Quaker, draws general philosophical consequences from the new physics:

> The physicist now regards his own external world in a way which I can only describe as more mystical, though not less exact and practical, than that which prevailed some years ago, when it was taken for granted that nothing could be true unless an engineer could make a model of it (Eddington, 1932: 344).

In *A World of Love*, ghost themes and fairy and folk tale merge with Biblical references, literary animism and the language of science and mysticism to indicate, in ways that lie beyond the scope of this study to investigate, alternative ways of seeing.

One figure left outside the general rejoicing at the end of *A World of Love* is Antonia. A celebrated photographer who can no longer find a subject, whose only marriage has failed, who seeks solace in alcohol, and who moves restlessly between London and County Cork, Antonia, solitary and uncertain over her future, does seem, as Corcoran suggests, to be 'a kind of black self-portrait of the artist in advancing age' (Corcoran, 2004: 77). Judging by photographs and letters from Bowen in this decade, Antonia's bedside table resembles what one imagines Bowen's to have been, namely a jumble of cigarettes, matches, sunglasses, 'a glass with dregs' (*WL*: 10), and, tellingly, a Bible. Antonia's loss of creative inspiration as a photographer finds its parallel in Bowen's admission that after Alan's death with the consequent loss of his pension, money worries 'the more deep for being repressed, increasingly slowed down my power to write, and it was upon my earnings, and those only, that Bowen's Court had by now come to depend' (*BC*: 458). Antonia is a prequel to Bowen's portrait of ageing women in her next novel.

The Little Girls (1964)

The late 1950s was a time of personal crisis for Bowen. There are ominous references in her correspondence to sessions with her bank manager about her overdraft and in a letter of 16 June 1958 from Rome she was obliged to ask Ritchie to send money (*LCW*: 308). A week later she wrote to him: 'One fact I'm facing: I *can't* go on carrying Bowen's Court. I'll have to get out of it somehow ... the house has become one great barrack of anxiety' (*LCW*: 309). By selling up not only was she, as she felt, letting down the generations of Bowens who had lived in Bowen's Court, she was also ending the dream that one day she and Ritchie would live there together. For a writer as attached to place as Bowen, the loss was devastating. In *The Death of the Heart* she had written: 'the destruction of buildings and furniture is more palpably dreadful to the spirit than the destruction of human life' for 'these things are what we mean when we speak of civilisation' (*DH*: 207). The threat had been there from the start in her experience, as an Anglo-Irishwoman, of an identity *in vacuo*, but in Victoria Glendinning's view the sale of Bowen's Court brought Bowen closer to the precipice than ever before: 'because of her father, [Bowen] was more afraid than most people of mental illness. In the crisis over Bowen's Court she drew as near to it herself as she was ever to get' (Glendinning, 1978: 276).

For a few months in 1959 Bowen drifted from place to place staying with friends, for all practical purposes homeless and, until the sale of Bowen's Court went through, in financial difficulties. Despite the jaunty façade she tried to maintain in her letters to Ritchie during this time, Bowen's loneliness and vulnerability break through. As a woman brought up in an age when women's purpose was to marry, and having relied on Alan's practical help throughout their marriage, she admitted she found organising her life difficult:

> Look at my life since Alan died – when I'm not with you I simply go drifting from one orbit of influence to another … I am slightly independent in my mind, that is, in my intellectual part – but quite outstandingly the reverse in disposition and temperament (*LCW*: 350).

She added tellingly: 'People make a mistake when they identify the performance I give with my real being' (*LCW*: 351).

The sale of Bowen's Court went through at the end of 1959, while Bowen was teaching at the American Academy in Rome, and the editors of her correspondence note that Ritchie did not keep any of her letters written between December 1959 and November 1960. As it was Ritchie's habit to suppress letters he felt were too exposing, one can only guess at the emotional turmoil expressed in Bowen's correspondence at this time. The sense of a widow astray is palpable in her travel memoir, *A Time in Rome* (1960), less guidebook than a record of confusion and loneliness in a city that constantly evades her attempts to find a home in it (Walshe, 2009: 152). 'To be dispossessed is horrible', she wrote, in the context of Cicero pleading for the restoration of his home (*TR*: 115). Eventually friends and relations helped sort out her financial affairs while Isaiah Berlin found her a flat in Oxford. It was here that she finished *The Little Girls*, a novel that in its Proustian working out of the theme of involuntary memory provides an analogy to the series of losses Bowen had sustained in recent years.

Bowen's decision to place three ageing women at the centre of *The Little Girls* was, in the context of the 1960s, with its emphasis on youth and sexual liberation, mildly subversive. Even feminism, faintly stirring in the early 1960s, would take several decades to engage positively with the ageing woman in works such as Germaine Greer's *The Change: Women, Ageing and the Menopause* (1991) and Betty Friedan's *The Fountain of Age* (1993). The novel's emotional force comes from the relationship between Dinah, Clare and Sheila, who were friends at school, lost touch in the intervening fifty or so years, and have now reached 'the days after' love (*LG*: 56). The tripartite structure moves from the present in the early 1960s to 1914 and back again to the present, in order to portray, in Bowen's words, three 'encaged, rather terrible little girls battering about inside grown-up (indeed, almost old) women' (*LCW*: 398). The middle section recreates the years that Bowen spent with her mother wandering from villa to villa on the Kent coast, making each new place a 'pavilion of love' until her mother's death brought this childhood idyll to an end (*MT*: 279–80). The ambivalent position of Florence Bowen as a woman living on her own with her child while her husband was in an Irish asylum, evolves in the novel into Mrs Piggott's uncertain social status, her husband's suicide and the unacknowledged love between herself and Major Burkin-Jones, Clare's father.

Though Dinah has a loyal male friend, Frank, male characters are marginal in *The Little Girls* and Ritchie, whose marriage Bowen continued to resent, interpreted 'the chilly exhilaration' of *The Little Girls* as 'revenge on love. Revenge on me' (*LCW*: 405). Possibly he was right. The editors of Bowen's letters to Ritchie note:

> She had many 'girl-friends' of a certain age, mainly in Sussex and Kent, some of them emotionally linked, whom she met frequently. CR was not told much about this aspect of her social life (*LCW*: 358).

Bowen did tell Ritchie, however, about a trip she made to Jordan in March 1964, before the book's publication, with her friend, Jean Black:

> In a way, this time here is being like an additional chapter to *The Little Girls*. I mean, our vocabulary and our recreations and our mental level seem to be about the same (as those of the Little G's, I mean) (*LCW*: 422).

At this point in her life, female friendships represented for Bowen a means of turning back the clock, to the days before marriage, when she attended girls' schools in the south of England, Lindum House, Harpenden Hall and Downe House, all of which she drew on for her portrait of St Agatha's in *The Little Girls*. At Harpenden Hall, the school she attended directly after her mother died, she took part in a burying episode, similar to the one in *The Little Girls* – 'a smallish biscuit tin, sealed, containing some cryptic writings and accompanied by two or three broken knick-knacks' (*MT*: 295). Anne Wyatt-Brown perceptively links this incident to unresolved mourning around her mother's death (Wyatt-Brown, 1993: 168–77).

In *The Little Girls*, originally to be called 'Race With Time' (*LCW:* 258), the central character's resistance to maturity recalls Oscar Wilde's *The Picture of Dorian Gray* (1891) and, as in Wilde's novel, the theme of time is interwoven with questions of aesthetics and the capacity of art to freeze time, a subject that also preoccupied the later Yeats. In the opening scene Dinah, with Frank's help, is preparing to bury objects donated by friends and neighbours in a time capsule, to be discovered and deciphered by posterity. The cave where they are engaged in this project seems suspended between past and future: 'Down here, however, it was some other hour – peculiar, perhaps no hour at all' (*LG*: 10). The suspension of time is reinforced by the drowsy atmosphere in Dinah's Somerset garden, as filled with warmth and sweet-scented flowers as Lord Henry's London garden in *Dorian Gray*. In this *Tír na nÓg* Dinah moves as though in a 'trance' (*LG*: 9).

The attempt to freeze a moment in time for posterity gathers further *Dorian Gray* overtones in the description of Dinah and Frank:

> A pair of ageless delinquents, whose random beauty was one of the most placid of their effronteries, or cheats: a cheating of Time. Nobody of their ages, it might be said, had any

business to look as these two still did. It could be that looking as they did was the something in common which had brought them together (*LG*: 12–13).

It becomes evident that these two are indeed trying to resist time, demonstrated in Frank's fear of becoming a grandfather and Dinah's inability, until the novel's conclusion, to let go of her childhood self. During the traumatic parting from Clare at the picnic in July 1914 that ends Part Two, the description of which is shot through with sinister references to the forthcoming war, it seems as though Clare has been spirited away by the *sidhe*, but it becomes clear that it is the immature Dinah who has remained trapped in endless youth.

Dinah's plan to bury objects expressive of people's personal obsessions is 'a race with time', an attempt to evade extinction of individuality in the future and to live on after death, a vanity project that is ironised from the beginning by Frank's observations that none of the objects is particularly distinctive and that, moreover, there may shortly be no future. As in all Bowen's works the personal context is shadowed by external events, here by references from Frank and Mrs Coral to the Cold War threat of nuclear annihilation that would render futile all of Dinah's plans for the future, reflecting contemporary anxieties about the survival of the planet, particularly acute in this period (Sturrock, 2009: 84). In Applegate some things do survive from the past – Mrs Piggott's fragile china, evoking for Clare a world of love that she has never managed to recreate in adult life, her embroidered footstools, an ivory Chinese puzzle, a French clock – but in the Cold War era survival into the future can never be taken for granted.

In the midst of this project Dinah experiences a disturbing flashback to a moment at school when she and two friends buried objects significant to them in a coffer for posterity to find, another arbitrary attempt to impose on the future. Frank warns her that her school friends will now be 'decidedly well-grown ladies' to which Dinah, still intent on evading time's erosions, responds: 'Don't be too sure' (*LG*: 23). *The Little Girls* endorses Dinah's belief in continuity with the past to the extent that when Dinah catches up with Clare and Sheila, all three revert to childhood roles and nicknames. 'Here they were, back where they had left off – how long ago? Not a day might have passed' (*LG*: 45). In 'Home for Christmas' (1955) Bowen argues that our first, youthful friendships 'are indissociable from our own identities; they colour life for us, and the colour stays' (*PPT*: 139). The novel suggests that an important part of the little girls' identities has been left behind with their abrupt parting from each other on the eve of the First World War, that historical rupture in the lives of all Bowen's contemporaries. In *The Little Girls*, the war is to kill Clare's father, seriously impact the health of Sheila's future lover (another oblique reference to Alan), and in the Spanish flu pandemic carry off Dinah's mother. Continuity with the past is further shaken when, after Dinah has suggested digging up the coffer, now that time has caught up with them and they themselves have become posterity, Sheila informs her friends that St Agatha's was shelled during the Second World War and no longer exists. Part One ends ominously on Clare's echo of *The Tempest* Act 4, scene 1: 'Into thin air' (*LG*: 63).

In Part Three, when Dinah, helped by Sheila and Clare, unearths the coffer buried in the grounds of what was formerly St Agatha's, the loss of its contents propels her into a nervous collapse similar to that Bowen herself experienced around the time of the sale of Bowen's Court:

> 'Yes, but I have to get back.'
> 'Your home', pointed out Sheila, 'won't run away.'
> Dinah examined the speaker, before saying: 'That's what it *has* done, Sheikie.' She took a shaky gulp at her drink. She added: 'Everything has. *Now* it has, you see. Nothing's real any more …
> We saw there was nothing *there*. So, where am I now?' (*LG*: 163).

On the evening of the discovery of the empty coffer Dinah, disorientated, attempts to cling to anything that seems changeless – Clare, Ravenswood Gardens. But at Sheila's house she discovers that more of the past has vanished and is forced into the Yeatsian realisation that art is a sterile counter to the richness of life in time. Standing in front of Sheila's bad watercolour of Southstone Old High Street, where the little girls used to spend their Saturday afternoons, Dinah learns that the street, bombed during the war, has been torn down and replaced. The painting seems to her a lie 'because it's here when the street is not' (*LG*: 169), in the same way as Dorian Gray feared his portrait would come to seem a lie as his face revealed time's depredations on his beauty. 'It might be better to have no picture of places which are gone', Dinah observes. 'Let them go completely' (*LG*: 169). It was literature's capacity to portray time that led Wilde, pursuing his argument with Whistler, to argue, in 'The Critic as Artist', for the superiority of literature over painting: 'Movement, that problem of the visual arts, can be truly realized by Literature alone. It is Literature that shows us the body in its swiftness and the soul in its unrest' (Wilde, 1972: 24). Unlike the painting of Southstone, Bowen's novel, by employing a tripartite structure, is able to capture the passage of time and its effect on a generation who lived through two world wars only to be threatened with nuclear annihilation.

Her two friends mirror, in a minor key, Dinah's struggle with time, ageing and death. Clare's sturdy body and ageing face proclaim a woman who has not tried to resist time's inroads: 'Bags underhung her eyes; deep creases, down from the broadened lobes of the nostrils, bracketed her mouth' (*LG*: 32). Yet even she reveals a wish to cling to the past, with her questions about Mrs Piggott, whom she loved in preference to her own cauterizing mother, and about her china, which has influenced the direction of her life and career to the extent that she has suspended time by recreating the atmosphere of Feverel Cottage in each of her Mopsie Pye shops. In these shops, customers move around, as if in a trance, buying the ephemeral, culturally appropriative bric-à-brac characteristic of 1960s consumer society. Sheila shows more of a wish to hold back time, in her face – 'The flesh of her face had hardened, perhaps through the effort involved in resisting change' (*LG*: 32) – her fashionable clothes, dyed hair, sporty car, and flirtatious manner. Yet Sheila has weathered sufficient setbacks in her life – the thwarting of her dreams of becoming a dancer, the death of her lover, unwanted infertility – to make her realistic about death and loss, and to regard Dinah with envy as having 'never yet outgrown being a selfish child' (*LG*: 174).

Though initially suspicious that Dinah is playing another of her emotional blackmail games, Clare eventually comes to understand the reasons for her friend's breakdown. She learns that Dinah's life has not been as safe as she had imagined: her father took his own life, she and her mother never returned to Feverel Cottage, she never replaced St Agatha's with any other school, she herself was widowed early and, as becomes clear, her unimaginative sons have no empathy with mental fragility. While Frank does possess insight into the sources of Dinah's trauma, handsome, selfish and over-imaginative like Dinah herself, he too much resembles her to be able to help. Clare finally comprehends that her fear of being drawn into an emotional vortex and reawakening her confusing feelings of love for Mrs Piggott, has impeded her recognition of her crucial anchoring role in Dinah's life:

> There being nothing was what you were frightened of all the time, eh? Yes. Yes, it was terrible looking down into that empty box. I did not comfort you. Never have I comforted you. Forgive me (*LG*: 236).

Commentators have suggested that behind these words lie not only Bowen's breakdown after the sale and subsequent demolition of Bowen's Court but also the earlier loss of her mother, whose funeral she had not been allowed to attend and all mention of whom she had suppressed for years (Wyatt-Brown, 1993: 164–86; Ellmann, 2004: 199). Indeed, following Ritchie's observation that Bowen split herself into two when writing *The Death of the Heart* – into the younger Portia and the older Anna (*LCW*: 26) – so in this novel Bowen's physical appearance and ambivalent lesbianism find an echo in Clare, her childlessness, never worn on her sleeve, in Sheila, and the early loss of her mother and the mental fragility, inherited from her father, in Dinah.

Clare's final recognition of her importance in Dinah's life comes too late. Dinah's collapse produces a belated maturity, an acceptance that the past, her childhood self, her mother, Feverel Cottage, the contents of the coffer, have gone forever. Clare will never be Mumbo again. Telling Clare, 'the game's up' (*LG*: 162), Dinah acknowledges that she must abandon her 'self-protective infantilism' (Lee, 1999: 194) and start to grow into her adult identity. As a little girl she had attempted to influence the future by burying objects in a coffer. Meeting her two school friends again she had tried to recapture the past. Now she must abandon the futile 'race with time' and live in the present, accepting that she cannot impose her will on posterity.

The Little Girls contains some of Bowen's characteristic themes – orphans, girls' schools, bereavement, mental instability, time, trauma and memory, as well as hauntings, revenants and other intimations of the supernatural, not least in the repeated references to witches and *Macbeth* – but it also reveals Bowen's growing dissatisfaction with the style of her previous novels. If her earlier novels were imbued with influences ranging from Henry James and E. M. Forster to the modernism of Woolf and the interwar fiction of Henry Green, Rosamond Lehmann and Graham Greene, Bowen's reading of contemporary writers like Evelyn Waugh and Muriel Spark led her, in a shift that disconcerted early critics, to move away in *The Little Girls* from modernist interiority towards dialogue and action as revelatory of character. The reading experience is complicated in Bowen's case since her characters remain of a Jamesian subtlety but now their complex feelings, instead of being explained to the reader in passages of controlled commentary, have to be revealed through gesture and pared-down, contemporary dialogue. 'Speech is what the characters *do to each other*', she wrote in 'Notes on Writing a Novel' (*MT*: 41).

Edward Said's term 'late style', indicating the intransigence, difficulties and contradictions evident in the aesthetic productions of some ageing artists, writers and composers (Said, 2006), is rarely applied to works by women but is appropriate for this penultimate novel in Bowen's career which, far from providing a rounded summation of her work, explores new directions and raises new questions for her readers. The style, often uncertain and open-ended, and deliberately experimental and exploratory, points to the fractured postmodernism of her final novel, *Eva Trout*, in which the reliability both of language and of human identity will be put under pressure.

Eva Trout, or Changing Scenes (1968)

By the time she had begun to write *Eva Trout*, Bowen had moved from Oxford to her last home, in Hythe on the Kent coast where she had lived with her mother as a child and which featured in the middle section of *The Little Girls*. Though her final novel seems to break free of Ireland, readers have discerned Anglo-Irish resonances in the depiction of the outsize heiress, Eva Trout, the last of her line, the most vulnerable and damaged of Bowen's orphans and also, in her yearning to achieve ordinary human life, the most disruptive of the lives of those around her, 'a Typhoid Mary', Henry Dancey calls her (*ET*: 179). In *Pictures and Conversations*, Bowen confesses that as a child in Kent, sharing a governess with a vicarage family (the Salmons, model for the Dancey family in *Eva Trout*) faced with the tameness of 'genuinely idyllic family life', she could not help behaving like a Swiftian 'yahoo', with a 'belligerence' she attributes to her Anglo-Irish ancestry (*MT*: 273–4).

If aspects of Eva's early life recall Bowen's own dislocated youth, they also mirror the betrayal and exploitation of Anglo-Irish children corralled into a narrative they have not chosen, as Margot Backus describes in *The Gothic Family Romance* (1999). The epistemological uncertainties of Anglo-Irish children faced with silences and gaps in the official colonial narratives are reflected in Eva's suspicion of Constantine's version of her childhood spent in the company of himself and his masochistic lover, her father, Willy Trout. Constantine himself may be read as an up-dating and parody of the wicked guardian figure of Anglo-Irish Gothic fiction who, in Eva's eyes, tormented her father to his death. The shadow cast over Eva's life by her father's helplessness in the face of Constantine's cruelty, an object correlative for Henry Bowen's periods of insanity, is made explicit by Iseult in her 'confession' to the camp High Church Anglican priest, Father Clavering-Haight: 'She had had enough of her father's vulnerability. She had watched him being destroyed' (*ET*: 243).

In *A Time in Rome*, Bowen traced the connection between alienation and a desire to take on the colour of one's surroundings:

> Anywhere, at any time, with anyone, one may be seized by the suspicion of being alien – ease is therefore to be found in a place which nominally *is* foreign: this shifts the weight ... one does not, it is true, belong, but one can imitate (*TR*: 27).

With her fake honeymoon in a beloved but dilapidated castle, her 'mimicry' of motherhood with her adopted child, Jeremy, and finally her wedding departure with Henry, Eva, seeking to fit into the proscribed life for a woman, stages her life as a series of imitative performances, recalling Bowen's description of Anglo-Irish lives as possessing 'something of the trance-like quality of a spectacle' (*MT*: 276). Eva, more than any other Bowen character, displays what Bowen described in *Bowen's Court* as her family's dangerous propensity to shape life to their fantasies (*BC*: 454–5), a trait she believed was shared with other Anglo-Irish after the Act of Union deprived them of power (*BC:* 258). The theme of fantasy colliding with reality, which can be traced throughout Bowen's novels, reaches its apogee in the final scene of *Eva Trout*.

The concept of 'late style' could appropriately be applied to *Eva Trout* since the novel, which disrupts both the notion of stable human identity and the reliability of language, offers a breathtakingly distorting perspective on Bowen's earlier work. She herself referred to *Eva Trout* as the 'inverse' of *The Death of the Heart*: 'everything turned upside down, so that the weights shift. One might say like a sand-glass reversed, so that the sand is flowing the *other* way' (*LCW:* 424). If the opening scenes where Iseult and Eva, an unwelcome guest in the Arble household, struggle like Anna and Portia for control over the script for their lives, the novel develops in unpredictable ways. Themes that lurked in the background of Bowen's earlier work, such as disability, homosexuality, lesbianism, adoption, language versus silence, come to the fore in *Eva Trout*. Under the impact of living through the cultural upheavals of the 1960s on American campuses, Bowen explores what it would be like to live, like Eva, in a world with no ethical framework, propelled by chaotic and unpredictable whims, and where visual spectacle (popular movies, television) replaces the linguistic challenges of great literature.

Bowen had firsthand knowledge of coping with disability on account of her severe stammer that developed around the time of her father's breakdown. She also had a deaf uncle, George, her mother's eldest brother, who played a major part in their lives in Dublin and Kent (*BC:* 406). Later in life, both her stepmother and her cousin Audrey Fiennes, one of her closest friends, went deaf. Bowen's fiction is full of characters disabled in major or minor ways: Daventry's shell shock, Kelway's limp, Harrison's uneven gaze, Francis' squint in *The Little Girls*, the 'slow' Annabelle in 'The Last Night in the Old Home', the simpleminded Anglo-Irish heiress, Valeria Cuffe in 'Her Table Spread'. Queenie's deafness in the wartime story 'Summer Night' is, as Maren Linett argues, both isolating and insightful. It is linked to an alternative way of seeing that allows her to plumb depths to an extent that unnerves her highly articulate brother, Justin, by intuiting what his sophisticated chatter is designed to conceal (Linett, 2013a: 465–93). Similarly, Bowen described her uncle George as someone who 'read character and sized up a situation with almost disconcerting exactitude' (*BC*: 406). In *Eva Trout* the visual intelligence of Jeremy who, like Bowen's uncle, relies on lip-reading, has the capacity to disconcert Mr Dancey and his son, Henry. Bowen was ahead of her time in treating disability sympathetically and in suggesting that the disabled might develop compensating abilities.

Eva's problems with language and social interaction have been read as both inherent, the result of a neurological disorder resembling autism (O'Brien, 2019: 75–93), and as caused by her social environment, in particular her disrupted childhood, wandering from country to country with her wealthy businessman father, Willy, and his sadistic lover, Constantine. Estranged from the nurturing possibilities of her remaining extended family, aunts and uncles who disapprove of Willy's relationship with Constantine, Eva spends much of her childhood in luxury hotels in the company of hired foreign carers, supplemented from time to time by governesses Willy telephones down for. Though such a lifestyle might have been an opportunity for Eva to develop as a cosmopolitan polyglot (Ellmann, 2004: 204), for Bowen who insisted in 'The Idea of Home' (1953) that 'identity would be nothing without its frame' (*LI*: 163), these dislocations do not provide Eva with an environment where either language or identity can develop naturally: 'unaided, she was beset by the quandaries of the rootless rich, for whom each choice becomes a vagary' (*ET*: 191). Like that other innocent, Prince Myshkin, Eva's long years of isolation from ordinary human life turn her into a wrecking ball for the society around her. By the time she arrives at Lumleigh school and encounters Iseult, a gifted teacher who recognizes Eva's difficulty in adapting to language, it is too late. Eva speaks in a way that forms a barrier to communication: 'she was unable to speak – talk, be understood, converse' (*ET*: 63). Echoing attempts by Bowen's governess, Miss Clark, to get her to conquer her stammer (*MT*: 272), Iseult encourages Eva to think rationally: 'Try joining things together: this, then that, then the other. That's thinking; at least, that's beginning to think' (*ET*: 62).

The opening of Chapter Five, giving an insight into Eva's non-linear, non-linguistic thought processes, reveals that while Eva thinks creatively in patterns, colours and visual images, she lacks the words to give her inner life meaning. Though this might be read as Eva compensating for her disability in the same way as Jeremy later compensates by fashioning intricate patterns out of fragments from the vicarage ash-heap, Bowen makes clear that both Eva and eventually Jeremy inspired by Iseult, desire to enter language. Eva's last words are to enquire about the meaning of 'concatenation', while Jeremy under the Bonnards' tutelage, pursues his speech exercises with rigour and determination. In a talk on language given in America in the late 1950s or early 1960s, Bowen argued: 'I am convinced that there *is*, in people, *a fundamental desire to be articulate* and that *inarticulateness* is the cause of *damage and pain*' (*LI*: 177). She knew from personal experience how stressful even a momentary inability to express oneself could be.

Inability to communicate takes different forms and *Eva Trout* is, as John Coates has argued, a brilliant satire on the emptiness and needless obfuscations of language employed by the supposedly sophisticated and articulate, chiefly Iseult, Constantine and Professor Holman whose letter to Eva is a triumph of meaningless verbiage (Coates, 1998: 240). Constantine, like his model, the Baron de Charlus, is self-regarding and prone to ponderous speeches, as in his internally contradictory final speech to Eva's assembled wedding guests where he borrows one of Charlus' favourite phrases, 'concatenation of circumstances'. In Iseult,

Bowen satirizes the effect of too much reading on a cerebral woman. Led astray by her enthusiasm for D. H. Lawrence, Iseult makes a Lawrentian marriage to her intellectual inferior, turns her love of Dickens into idolatry, likening him to Christ, and pitches her own literary ambitions too high, writing a novel that is 'born dead' (*ET*: 228). In the final scene, when Iseult and Eric, apparently reconciled, arrive at Victoria Station, they have dwindled into a dull, provincial couple. Iseult, whose imagination has been deadened by contact with too many books, gazes in awe at Eva who, boldly enacting her riskiest fantasy yet, stands 'luminous from top to toe' (*ET*: 262).

Eva, even more maternally bereft than Lois – her sole memory of her dead mother is a 'shriek' (*ET*: 40) – shares Lois' intense feelings for women. Bowen's interrogation of gender and sexual identities in *Eva Trout* has been explored notably by Tina O'Toole (O'Toole, 2009: 162–78), Patricia Juliana Smith (1997) and Renée Hoogland (1994). At the boarding school for wealthy delinquents financed by Willy as a means of separating Constantine from Kenneth his rival, Eva feels united in a moment outside time with her roommate Elsinore, abandoned in a coma by the school authorities: 'This deathly yet living stillness, together, of two beings, this unapartness, came to be the requital of all longing' (*ET*: 56). This return-to-the-womb interlude is broken off when Elsinore's mother arrives to take her daughter away.

In her unmothered, homeless state, Eva misinterprets the 'vivisectional' attention Iseult pays to her at Lumleigh as love. As obsessional as her father, she quickly exhausts Iseult's never very strong capacity to nurture. Like Anna in Kate O'Brien's *The Land of Spices* (1941), Eva recites a passage of seventeenth-century metaphysical poetry, transferring the love of God in the poem to love of her teacher. But, unlike the Reverend Mother whose heart is flooded with emotion by Anna's recital, Iseult resists Eva's feelings by coldly analysing the prosody. Recognising that she has taken on a task beyond her powers, Iseult abandons her task, forever after resenting Eva on that account and leaving Eva's identity unformed. As Eva explains later to Father Clavering-Haight, she hoped Iseult would teach her how 'to be, to become – I had never been', but Iseult 'sent me back again – to be nothing ... I remain gone. Where am I? I do not know' (*ET*: 185). From now on, Eva will buy her way into human life. She moves to Broadstairs, to a house named Cathay, which she fills with the latest audiovisual aids for communication, relying on technology to complete the task Iseult abandoned. When Iseult comes to visit, Eva informs her that she is intending to purchase a computer in order to teach herself how to think and enacts revenge on the unhappily childless Iseult by claiming to be pregnant by Eric.

Eva's determination to bend the world to her wishes by writing herself into a maternal script encounters an obstacle when, heartbreakingly, Jeremy, the baby Eva adopts (or rather buys illegally), and who in her words 'was to be everything I shall not be' (*ET*: 199), turns out to be a deaf-mute. Since Jeremy inhabits a world of silence, he is no help in pulling Eva into language. Maren Linett notes that Eva's failure to supply Jeremy with sign language, while historically plausible, increases their isolation (Linett, 2013b: 277). For eight years mother and son live together in pre-oedipal, wordless communication, feeding off images provided by contemporary society:

> His and her cinematographic existence, with no sound-track, in successive American cities made still more similar by their continuous manner of being in them, had had a sufficiency which was perfect. Sublimated monotony had cocooned the two of them, making them as near as twins in a womb (*ET*: 188).

In the movie-world that Eva and Jeremy inhabit, boundaries between illusion and reality, between self and other, are dissolved; Eva has finally achieved the symbiotic bond that she had previously longed for with Elsinore. There is a faint echo here of Bowen's 'dreamlike drives' as a child with her deaf uncle George (*BC*: 406).

Returning to England with Jeremy, Eva's rejection of the world of language and civilization begins to soften:

> The fact was, since her return to England her mistrust of or objection to verbal intercourse — which she had understood to be fundamental — began to be undermined … She was ready to talk (*ET*: 188).

Falling in love with Henry, she longs to enter his articulate Cambridge world and, in the face of his hesitations, arranges to go through a pretend form of marriage with him. Eva understands desire but not responsibility: in Chicago she rejected the weeping Elsinore's overtures, being now focused on buying a baby. She discounts the fact that by moving out of the wordless, pre-oedipal bond with Jeremy, she is betraying their years together: 'She had not computed the cost for him of entry into another dimension' (*ET*: 189).

Eva's determination to move people around according to her wishes mirrors the novelist organising her/his fictional world and echoes something Bowen discovered about herself during the course of her first love affair, with Humphry House:

> One may – I may – easily forget that a relationship with a person isn't a book, created out of, projected by, one's own imagination and will. That it is not, in fact, a one-man show (Glendinning, 1978: 110).

Bowen continued to the end of her life to display ruthlessness in her love affairs. Her letters to Ritchie reveal her, at times, to be keeping their affair alive through sheer will power and invention, and her behaviour towards Sylvia, Ritchie's wife, could be chillingly manipulative (*LCW*: 438). Eva's great wealth gives her power over people's lives akin to that of the novelist and, obsessed with Henry, she replicates with Jeremy Willy's callous behaviour towards herself.

As so often in Bowen's work (in *The House in Paris*, in the short stories 'The Tommy Crans' and 'The Little Girl's Room'), to the extent that it comes to seem like an argument she was having with herself, adoption ends in failure. Eva breaks her promise to Jeremy to provide him with a home and he returns from their abortive visit to Cathay bereft. In a phrase from *Hebrews* 13:14 that resonates through Bowen's work, he lacks an 'abiding city' (*ET*: 163). Jeremy's growing hostility to Eva, expressed visually in the sculptured head he models of her, its sightless eyes exuding 'non-humanity' (*ET*: 190), turns his mother into the abject, an object of horror, in order to facilitate separation from her. Whether provoked by a desire to avenge herself on Eva, or by a wish to succeed with Jeremy where she failed with Eva, Iseult aids this process of separation by kidnapping Jeremy for a few hours and encouraging him into the world of language.

Motivated by his time spent with Iseult, Jeremy willingly submits to treatment by French doctors, the Bonnards, who give him language (significantly French rather than Eva's mother tongue, English), and therefore access to wider knowledge than could be gleaned from his previous dependence on two-dimensional visual images on television screens and in films. With Jeremy's discovery of language and his first efforts at speech, comes resentment of the shady transaction by which Eva acquired him in the first place. What is between them is not a flesh and blood tie, he realizes, only a simulacrum of the mother-child relationship: 'Like as they were, they were *not* of each other's flesh-and-blood, and they both knew it. The dear game was over, the game was up' (*ET*: 254). Like Leopold in *The House in Paris*, Jeremy repudiates his adopted family and begins to develop a self apart from his mother, entering a masculine, public world symbolized by his new dispatch case: 'About his entrance there was already a touch of the executive, however junior' (*ET*: 254). Justifying the narrator's observation that handicaps can be a spur to achievement (*ET*: 256), Jeremy, like Leopold, is determined to conquer the adult world.

It is Henry's decision to remain with Eva that brings Eva to life. She bursts into tears, the very first tears she has ever shed, at last moving beyond spectacle and fantasy into the human condition and suggesting the error of her belief that the pictures in the National Portrait Gallery confirmed there are no such things as human beings with interior lives. However, Eva is not given a chance to develop her humanity since, in an appropriately cinematic ending, Jeremy guns her down. Bowen leaves it open to interpretation whether Jeremy's act is accidental or intentional. If accidental it reinforces the theme of Eva's life as a haphazard collection of 'changing scenes' and life as an unjust affair of faulty scales, to borrow from the title of Mr Dancey's endlessly unfinished book. If intentional, Jeremy's action looks like retribution, the last act in a 'concatenation' of events that began with Eva's original sin of adopting him, thus diverting the course of his destiny: 'one does not do such a thing with impunity, the priest had said. The doctor had warned her...' (*ET*: 233). Her very public departure with Henry is an ostentatious abandonment of him. Madame Bonnard whose own childlessness is sketched out with Bowen's characteristic terseness on this subject – 'Madame Bonnard had had to school herself to one kind of abstinence: as to "mothering". The Bonnards had no children' (*ET*: 221) – warns Eva that, despite his wish for separation, there remains much in their relationship for Jeremy to feel hurt about: 'It is still in your power to offend him' (*ET*: 258).

Biblical and Christian allusions abound in *Eva Trout*: Eden, apples, the Fall, the Virgin Mary, Abraham's sacrifice, the law of the Old Testament, the echo of a familiar hymn in the subtitle, among others. Like the myriad literary references throughout the novel, these allusions do not, as Neil Corcoran notes, cohere into any consistent pattern but are simply, as in a postmodernist novel, left hanging (Corcoran, 2004: 136–8). Christian references may, however, be intended by the author to point up an alternative to the radical social and political upheavals of the 1960s. For some of the characters they do possess meaning: for Reverend Dancey, for Father Clavering-Haight, and for Constantine after his conversion, the genuineness of which may account for his sudden character change between Part One and Part Two, something found perplexing by many readers. In keeping with Bowen's belief in the intelligence of her readers, we are never coerced into accepting one interpretation over another and in fact for a character like Eva it is part of Bowen's point about the society in which she lives that Christianity, like good literature, is an irrelevance. There are resonances here with Woolf's *The Years* (1937) with its vision of a future where knowledge is fragmented and language fails. That Eva herself never resolves her difficulties with language, meaning and connection is reflected in her final words: '"Constantine," asked Eva, "what is concatenation?"' (*ET*: 268).

Eva's frantic dash through life, using 'mindless speed' as 'armour' (*ET*: 142), resembles Bowen's own last decade forever on the move between Europe and the States and sometimes, especially around the time of the sale of Bowen's Court, like Eva, maintaining a silence that distressed her friends and relatives (Laurence, 2019: 289). Eva's inability to use words and make ethical connections, relying on lies and fantasies in lieu, suggests Bowen's all too prescient fears for what humans might become in a society based on consumption, simulation and spectacle. With it comes a warning that humans are in danger of losing their humanity: Eva's resemblance to a robot or cyborg has often been noted by critics (O'Toole, 2009: 168–9; Ellmann, 2004: 209). Bowen's final creation is brilliantly prophetic about the way in which society was to evolve by the end of the twentieth century.

The technological future Bowen conjures up in her final novel, *Eva Trout*, is a far cry from the Anglo-Irish world of *The Last September*, but the same themes of identity, language and alienation continued to preoccupy her at the end of her writing life as at the beginning, even if the society she portrayed had radically altered.

Epilogue

Any attempt to sum up Bowen's multi-layered and protean body of work would be premature at this stage, when so many new avenues of research are being explored by young scholars all over the world. This epilogue aims simply to sketch out some possible avenues for future research.

The publication of her revealing, occasionally unnerving, letters to Charles Ritchie, has highlighted Bowen's complex and many-sided personality. There is still much to be explored around the themes of childlessness and adopted children in her fiction. Critical work has begun on trauma (Gildersleeve 2014) and disability (Linett 2013) in her writing, but again, both these topics lend themselves to further exploration. Given Bowen's roots as a countrywoman, the time is perhaps ripe for ecocritical approaches to her work, looking not only at her portrayal of landscapes (Walshe, 2019), but at the part played by gardens, flowers and trees in her writing. Even in her direst economic crises, she was tenacious in her refusal to cut down timber on the Bowen demesne, conservationist values she inherited from her father (Laurence, 2019: 67–70).

In recent times, there has been a welcome opening up of critical debate around Bowen's engagement with the social and political issues of her day and a recognition that her political and social insights are far wider ranging than she used to be given credit for. Scope remains for further research in this area, notably an in-depth study of the figure of the refugee in Bowen's writing, developing the work of Phyllis Lassner and Paula Derdiger (2009), and Lyndsey Stonebridge (2011).

As discussed in the introduction and touched on at various points during this study, 'intelligent faith' in Bowen's work deserves closer inspection. In *The Death of the Heart*, Mrs Heccomb's church going is treated fondly by a writer familiar with the minor details of parish life, while in *Eva Trout* the Reverend Dancey is one of the few portraits in Bowen's fiction of a sympathetic male figure. The merging of Biblical references with ghost themes, literary animism and the language of science and mysticism is another way of approaching her work, following pioneering research by Jacqueline Rose (2000), Elizabeth Inglesby (2007), Sinéad Mooney (2009a), and Carissa Foo (2019), and is particularly relevant in the context of Bowen's short stories and of *A World of Love*.

The question of literary influences could not be explored in any depth in a brief study like this. There is much to be said about Bowen's borrowings, not only from modernist favourites such as Proust, Flaubert, James, Forster, Woolf and Mansfield, but from the Bible, Shakespeare, Dickens, Faulkner, D. H. Lawrence and others. In particular, it would be useful to have an account of the evolution of literary influences over the course of Bowen's career. Work on this has already begun: Diana Hirst (2018) has discussed Bowen's use of Hans Christian Anderson's *The Snow Queen* in *To the North* while Victoria Warren (1999) drew a detailed comparison between *The Death of the Heart* and Jane Austen's *Emma*, though she presses the correspondences closer than I would wish to – Bowen's use of literary sources was always fleeting, tangential, and suggestive rather than laboured.

There would be rewards in paying close attention to the ways in which Bowen's disruptive narratives achieve their complex stylistic effects, requiring of the reader constant alertness to the unexpected phrase or piercing insight. The influence of her early art training on the intense visual and sensory imagery in her work deserves a full-length study: in a 1950 interview she pointed to the importance of light effects in her writing (*LI*: 280). Her enthusiasm for the new media of photography and cinema, and for the avant-garde movements of Surrealism and Futurism, and the way these played into her literary style merit further exploration, building on the scholarship of Keri Walsh (2017, 2019) and Diana Hirst (2018). In an interview broadcast in 1959, Bowen agreed that her interest in architecture had influenced both her life and her writing (*LI*: 330–31). Elke D'hoker (2012) and Jasmin Kelaita (2019) have begun the study of domestic spaces in Bowen's writings. An investigation of the precise architectural observations in her fiction might yield further insights.

Much work remains to be done on this most elusive of writers, though there will always be an aspect of the unknown involved in our experience of reading Bowen, both the woman and her writing. Her inconclusive plots and stated preference for creating silences and mystery around her characters make resistance to final explanation an appropriate end note.

Select Bibliography

Primary Works by Elizabeth Bowen

Novels
1927. *The Hotel* (Harmondsworth: Penguin, 1987).
1929. *The Last September* (Harmondsworth: Penguin, 1987).
1931. *Friends and Relations* (Harmondsworth: Penguin, 1987).
1932. *To the North* (London: Vintage, 1999).
1935. *The House in Paris* (Harmondsworth: Penguin, 1987).
1938. *The Death of the Heart* (Harmondsworth: Penguin, 1989).
1949. *The Heat of the Day* (London: Vintage, 1998).
1955. *A World of Love* (London: Vintage, 1999).
1964. *The Little Girls* (Harmondsworth: Penguin, 1982).
1968. *Eva Trout, or Changing Scenes* (London: Vintage, 1999).

Short Story Collections
1932. *Encounters* (London: Sidgwick and Jackson).
1926. *Ann Lee's and Other Stories* (London: Sidgwick and Jackson).
1929. *Joining Charles and Other Stories* (London: Constable).
1934. *The Cat Jumps and Other Stories* (London: Gollancz).
1941. *Look At All Those Roses* (London: Gollancz).
1945. *The Demon Lover and Other Stories* (London: Cape). Published in the US as *Ivy Gripped the Steps and Other Stories* (New York: Knopf, 1946).
1951. *Early Stories: Encounters and Ann Lee's* (New York: Knopf).
1959. *Stories by Elizabeth Bowen* (New York: Vintage Books).
1965. *A Day in the Dark and Other Stories* (London: Cape).
1980. *Collected Stories* (London: Vintage, 1999).
2008. *The Bazaar and Other Stories* edited by Allan Hepburn (Edinburgh: Edinburgh University Press).

Non-Fiction

1937. Foreword to *The Faber Book of Modern Short Stories* in *The New Short Story Theories* edited by Charles May, 256–62 (Athens: Ohio University Press, 1994).
1942. *Bowen's Court and Seven Winters* (London: Virago, 1984).
1942. *English Novelists* (London: Collins).
1950. *Collected Impressions* (London: Longmans).
1951. *The Shelbourne* (London: Vintage, 2017).
1959. *A Time in Rome* (London: Vintage, 2010).
1962. *Afterthought: Pieces About Writing* (London: Longmans).
1975. *Pictures and Conversations* (London: Cape).
1986. *The Mulberry Tree: Writings of Elizabeth Bowen* edited by Hermione Lee (London: Vintage, 1999).
2008. *Love's Civil War* edited by Victoria Glendinning, with Judith Robertson (London: Simon and Schuster).
2008. *People, Places, Things: Essays by Elizabeth Bowen* edited by Allan Hepburn (Edinburgh: Edinburgh University Press).
2010. *Listening In: Broadcasts, Speeches, and Interviews by Elizabeth Bowen* edited by Allan Hepburn (Edinburgh: Edinburgh University Press).
2011. *Elizabeth Bowen's Selected Irish Writings* edited by Eibhear Walshe (Cork: Cork University Press).

Secondary Works

d'Alton, Ian. 2018. '"No More Autumns" – Elizabeth Bowen and an Anglo-Irish Imagery of Dying and Dead Houses'. *The Elizabeth Bowen Review* 1 (May): 19–30. http://www.bowensociety.com/wp-content/uploads/2017/05/The-Elizabeth-Bowen-Review-Volume-1-May-2018-1.pdf
Backus, Margot Gayle. 1999. *The Gothic Family Romance: Heterosexuality, Child Sacrifice, and the Anglo-Irish Colonial Order* (Durham, NC and London: Duke University Press).
Beauman, Nicola. 1983. *A Very Great Profession. The Woman's Novel 1914–39* (London: Virago).
Beddoe, Deirdre. 1989. *Women Between the Wars, 1918–1939: Back to Home and Duty* (London: Pandora Press).
Beer, Gillian. 1996. '"Wireless": Popular Physics, Radio and Modernism'. In *Cultural Babbage: Technology, Time and Invention* edited by Francis Spufford and Jenny Uglow, 149–66. (London: Faber and Faber).
Bence-Jones, Mark. 1987. *Twilight of the Ascendancy* (London: Constable).
Bennett, Andrew and Nicholas Royle. 1995. *Elizabeth Bowen and the Dissolution of the Novel* (Basingstoke: Macmillan).
Bennett, Andrew. 2009. 'Bowen and Modernism: The Early Novels'. In *Elizabeth Bowen* edited by Eibhear Walshe, 27–39. (Dublin: Irish Academic Press).
——. 2019. 'Elizabeth Bowen on the Telephone'. In *Elizabeth Bowen: Theory,*

Thought and Things edited by Jessica Gildersleeve and Patricia Juliana Smith, 182–98. (Edinburgh: Edinburgh University Press).

Bluemel, Kristin. 2009. *Intermodernism: Literary Culture in Mid-Twentieth-Century Britain* (Edinburgh: Edinburgh University Press).

Brassard, Geneviève. 2007. 'Fast and Loose in Interwar London: Mobility and Sexuality in Elizabeth Bowen's *To the North*'. *Women: A Cultural Review* 18 (3): 282–302.

Breen, Mary. 2009. '"Autobiography As We Know It Now Is Artists' Work"'. In *Elizabeth Bowen* edited by Eibhear Walshe, 110–32. (Dublin: Irish Academic Press).

Chessmann, Harriet. 1983. 'Women and Language in the Fiction of Elizabeth Bowen'. *Twentieth Century Literature* 29 (1): 69–85.

Christensen, Lis. 2001. *Elizabeth Bowen: The Later Fiction* (Copenhagen: Museum Tusculanum Press).

Coates, John. 1998. *Social Discontinuity in the Novels of Elizabeth Bowen: The Conservative Quest* (Lewiston: Edwin Mellen).

Cooper, Lettice. 1987. *The New House* (London: Virago).

Corcoran, Neil. 2004. *Elizabeth Bowen: The Enforced Return* (Oxford: Clarendon Press).

Coughlan, Patricia. 1997. 'Women and Desire in the Work of Elizabeth Bowen'. In *Sex, Nation and Dissent in Irish Writing* edited by Eibhear Walshe, 103–31. (Cork: Cork University Press).

——. 2018. 'Elizabeth Bowen'. In *A History of Modern Irish Women's Literature* edited by Heather Ingman and Cliona Ó Gallchoir, 204–226. (Cambridge: Cambridge University Press).

Cullingford, Elizabeth. 2007. '"Something Else": Gendering Onliness in Elizabeth Bowen's Early Fiction'. *Modern Fiction Studies* 53 (2): 276–305.

Darwood, Nicola. 2012. *A World of Lost Innocence: The Fiction of Elizabeth Bowen* (Newcastle upon Tyne: Cambridge Scholars).

D'hoker, Elke. 2012. 'The Poetics of House and Home in the Short Stories of Elizabeth Bowen'. *Orbis Litterarum* 67 (4): 267–89.

Eddington, Arthur S. 1932. *The Nature of the Physical World* (Cambridge: Cambridge University Press).

Ellmann, Maud. 2004. *Elizabeth Bowen: The Shadow Across the Page* (Edinburgh: Edinburgh University Press).

Foo, Carissa. 2019. 'Patriarchal Hauntings and Feminist Exorcisms in Elizabeth Bowen's Short Stories'. *The Elizabeth Bowen Review* 2 (September): 59–71. http://www.bowensociety.com/wp-content/uploads/2017/05/The-Elizabeth-Bowen-Review-Volume-2-September-2019.pdf

Foster, R. F. 1995. *Paddy and Mr Punch: Connections in Irish History and English History* (Harmondsworth: Penguin).

——. 2002. *The Irish Story: Telling Tales and Making It Up in Ireland* (Harmondsworth: Penguin).

Gan, Wendy. 2009. *Women, Privacy and Modernity in Early Twentieth-Century British Writing* (New York: Palgrave Macmillan).
Gay, Jane de. 2018. *Virginia Woolf and Christian Culture* (Edinburgh: Edinburgh University Press).
Gildersleeve, Jessica. 2014. *Elizabeth Bowen and the Writing of Trauma: the Ethics of Survival* (Amsterdam: Costerus New Series).
—— and Smith, Patricia Juliana, eds. 2019. *Elizabeth Bowen: Theory, Thought and Things* (Edinburgh: Edinburgh University Press).
Glendinning, Victoria. 1978. *Elizabeth Bowen* (New York: Alfred A. Knopf).
Harmon, Maurice. 1994. *Sean O'Faoláin* (London: Constable).
Hartley, Jenny. 1997. *Millions Like Us. British Women's Fiction of the Second World War* (London: Virago Press).
Hazelgrove, Jenny. 2000. *Spiritualism and British Society Between the Wars* (Manchester: Manchester University Press).
Hepburn, Allan. 2009. 'Trials and Errors: *The Heat of the Day* and Postwar Culpability'. In *Intermodernism: Literary Culture in Mid-Twentieth-Century Britain* edited by Kristin Bluemel, 131–149. (Edinburgh: Edinburgh University Press).
Hirst, Diana. 2018. 'Shaking the cracked kaleidoscope: Elizabeth Bowen's Use of Futurism and Collage in *To the North*'. *The Elizabeth Bowen Review* 1 (May): 63–74. http://www.bowensociety.com/wp-content/uploads/2017/05/The-Elizabeth-Bowen-Review-Volume-1-May-2018-1.pdf
Hobson, Suzanne. 2011. *Angels of Modernism: Religion, Culture, Aesthetics 1910–1960* (New York: Palgrave Macmillan).
Hoogland, Renée. 1994. *Elizabeth Bowen: A Reputation in Writing* (New York: New York University Press).
Hopkins, Chris. 2006. *English Fiction in the 1930s: Language, Genre, History* (London and New York: Continuum Literary Studies).
Inglesby, Elizabeth. 2007. '"Expressive Objects": Elizabeth Bowen's Narrative Materializes'. *Modern Fiction Studies* 53 (2): 306–333.
Ingman, Heather. 1998. *Women's Fiction Between the Wars: Mothers, Daughters and Writing* (Edinburgh: Edinburgh University Press).
——. 2007. *Twentieth-Century Fiction by Irish Women: Nation and Gender* (Burlington: Ashgate).
——. 2010a. '"Like Shakespeare," she added … "or isn't it": Shakespearean Echoes in Elizabeth Bowen's portrait of Ireland'. In *Shakespeare and the Irish Writer* edited by Janet Clare and Stephen O'Neill, 153–65. (Dublin: UCD Press).
——. 2010b. 'Religion and the occult in women's modernism'. In *The Cambridge Companion to Modernist Women Writers* edited by Maren Tova Linett, 187–202. (Cambridge: Cambridge University Press).
——. 2013. *Irish Women's Fiction: From Edgeworth to Enright* (Dublin: Irish Academic Press).
——. 2018. '"A Living Writer": Elizabeth Bowen and Katherine Mansfield'.

The Elizabeth Bowen Review 1 (May): 30–41. http://www.bowensociety.com/wp-content/uploads/2017/05/The-Elizabeth-Bowen-Review-Volume-1-May-2018-1.pdf

—— and Clíona Ó Gallchoir, eds. 2018. *A History of Modern Irish Women's Literature* (Cambridge: Cambridge University Press).

Joannou, Maroula. 1995. *'Ladies, Please Don't Smash These Windows'. Women's Writing, Feminist Consciousness and Social Change 1918–38* (Oxford: Berg).

—— ed. 2013. *The History of British Women's Writing, 1920–1945* (Basingstoke: Palgrave Macmillan).

Johnson, Kathryn. 2011. '"Phantasmagoric Hinterlands": Adolescence and Anglo-Ireland in Elizabeth Bowen's *The House in Paris* and *The Death of the Heart*'. In *Irish Women Writers* edited by Elke D'hoker, Raphael Ingelbien, Hedwig Schwall, 207–226. (Bern: Peter Lang).

Jordan, Heather Bryant. 1992. *How Will the Heart Endure? Elizabeth Bowen and the Landscape of War* (Ann Arbor, MI: University of Michigan Press).

——. 2008. 'A Bequest of Her Own: The Reinvention of Elizabeth Bowen'. *New Hibernia Review* 12 (2): 46–62.

Kelaita, Jasmin. 2019. 'Housekeeping and the Fiction of Subjectivity in *Eva Trout*'. In *Elizabeth Bowen: Theory, Thought and Things* edited by Jessica Gildersleeve and Patricia Juliana Smith, 165–81. (Edinburgh: Edinburgh University Press).

Kiberd, Declan. 1996. *Inventing Ireland: The Literature of the Modern Nation* (London: Vintage).

Kreilkamp, Vera. 1998. *The Anglo-Irish Novel and the Big House* (Syracuse: Syracuse University Press).

——. 2009. 'Bowen: Ascendancy Modernist'. In *Elizabeth Bowen* edited by Eibhear Walshe, 12–26. (Dublin: Irish Academic Press).

Laird, Heather. 2009. 'The "Placing" and Politics of Bowen in Contemporary Irish Literary and Cultural Criticism'. In *Elizabeth Bowen* edited by Eibhear Walshe, 193–207. (Dublin: Irish Academic Press).

Lassner, Phyllis. 1990. *Elizabeth Bowen* (Basingstoke: Macmillan).

——. 1991. *Elizabeth Bowen: A Study of the Short Fiction* (New York: Twayne).

——. and Paula Derdiger. 2009. 'Domestic Gothic, the Global Primitive, and Gender Relations in Elizabeth Bowen's *The Last September* and *The House in Paris*'. In *Irish Modernism and the Global Primitive* edited by Maria McGarrity and Claire Culleton, 195–214. (New York: Palgrave Macmillan).

Laurence, Patricia. 2019. *Elizabeth Bowen: A Literary Life*. (New York: Palgrave Macmillan).

Lee, Hermione. 1999. *Elizabeth Bowen* (London: Vintage).

Lewis, Pericles. 2010. *Religious Experience and the Modernist Novel* (Cambridge: Cambridge University Press).

Linett, Maren. 2007. *Modernism, Feminism and Jewishness* (Cambridge: Cambridge University Press).

——. 2013a. '"Seeing, seeing, seeing": Deafness, Knowledge and Subjectivity in

Elizabeth Bowen'. *Twentieth-Century Literature* 59 (3): 465–93.

———. 2013b. 'Modes of Dislocation: Jewishness and Deafness in Elizabeth Bowen'. *Studies in the Novel* 45 (2): 259–78.

Maude, Ulrika. 2019. 'Tender Ties: Elizabeth Bowen and Habit'. In *Elizabeth Bowen: Theory, Thought and Things* edited by Jessica Gildersleeve and Patricia Juliana Smith, 79–95. (Edinburgh: Edinburgh University Press).

McCormack, W. J. 1993. *Dissolute Characters: Irish Literary History through Balzac, Sheridan Le Fanu, Yeats and Bowen* (Manchester: Manchester University Press).

Melero, Layla Ferrández. 2019. '"There Was Certainly Something *in* the Girl": Sydney as Sapphist Character in Elizabeth Bowen's *The Hotel*'. *The Elizabeth Bowen Review* 2 (September): 71–84. http://www.bowensociety.com/wp-content/uploads/2017/05/The-Elizabeth-Bowen-Review-Volume-2-September-2019.pdf

Miller, Kristine A. 2010. *British Literature of the Blitz: Fighting the People's War* (Basingstoke: Palgrave Macmillan).

Minh-ha, Trinh T. 1994. 'Other than myself/my other self'. In *Travellers' Tales: Narratives of Home and Displacement* edited by George Robertson et al, 8–26. (London: Routledge).

Mooney, Sinéad. 2009a. 'Bowen and the Modern Ghost'. In *Elizabeth Bowen* edited by Eibhear Walshe, 77–94. (Dublin: Irish Academic Press).

———. 2009b. 'Unstable compounds: Bowen's Beckettian affinities'. In *Elizabeth Bowen: New Critical Perspectives* edited by Susan Osborn, 13–33. (Cork: Cork University Press).

Moynahan, Julian. 1995. *Anglo-Irish: The Literary Imagination in a Hyphenated Culture* (Princeton: Princeton University Press).

O'Brien, Valerie. 2019. '"A Genius for Unreality": Neurodiversity in Elizabeth Bowen's *Eva Trout*'. *Journal of Modern Literature* 42 (2): 75–93.

O'Faoláin, Sean. 1982. 'A Reading and Remembrance of Elizabeth Bowen'. *London Review of Books* 4 (4): 15–16.

Osborn, Susan ed. 2009. *Elizabeth Bowen: New Critical Perspectives* (Cork: Cork University Press).

O'Toole, Tina. 2009. 'Angels and Monsters: Embodiment and Desire in *Eva Trout*'. In *Elizabeth Bowen* edited by Eibhear Walshe, 162–78. (Dublin: Irish Academic Press).

Panter-Downes, Mollie. 2014. *London War-Notes* (London: Persephone Books).

Parkins, Wendy. 2001. 'Moving Dangerously: Mobility and the Modern Woman'. *Tulsa Studies* 20 (1): 77–92.

Pearson, Nels. 2015. *Irish Cosmopolitanism: Location and Dislocation in James Joyce, Elizabeth Bowen, and Samuel Beckett* (Gainesville: University Press of Florida).

Piette, Adam. 2017. 'War and the Short Story: Elizabeth Bowen'. In *British Women Short Story Writers: The New Woman to Now* edited by Emma Young and James Bailey, 66–80. (Edinburgh: Edinburgh University Press).

Plain, Gill. 1996. *Women's Fiction of the Second World War: Gender, Power and Resistance* (Edinburgh: Edinburgh University Press).

Radford, Jean. 1999. 'Late Modernism and the Politics of History'. In *Women Writers of the 1930s: Gender, Politics and History* edited by Maroula Joannou, 33–45. (Edinburgh: Edinburgh University Press).
Rose, Jacqueline. 2000. 'Bizarre Objects: Mary Butts and Elizabeth Bowen.' *Critical Quarterly* 42 (1): 75–85.
Said, Edward. 2006. *On Late Style: Music and Literature Against the Grain* (New York and London: Bloomsbury).
Smith, Patricia Juliana. 1997. *Lesbian Panic: Homoeroticism in Modern British Women's Fiction* (New York: Columbia University Press).
Stevens, Julie Anne. 2009. 'Bowen: The Critical Response'. In *Elizabeth Bowen* edited by Eibhear Walshe, 179–192. (Dublin: Irish Academic Press).
Stevenson, John. 1990. *British Society 1914–45* (Harmondsworth: Penguin).
Stewart, Victoria. 2009. 'Violence and Representation in Elizabeth Bowen's Interwar Short Stories'. *English* (58): 139–59.
Stonebridge, Lyndsey. 2011. *The Judicial Imagination: Writing After Nuremberg* (Edinburgh: Edinburgh University Press).
Sturrock, June. 2009. 'Mumbo-jumbo: the haunted world of *The Little Girls*'. In *Elizabeth Bowen: New Critical Perspectives* edited by Susan Osborn, 83–95. (Cork: Cork University Press).
Teekell, Anna. 2011. 'Elizabeth Bowen and Language at War'. *New Hibernia Review* 15 (3): 61–79.
———. 2018. *Emergency Writing: Irish Literature, Neutrality, and the Second World War* (Evanston: Northwestern University Press).
Thurschwell, Pamela. 2001. *Literature, Technology, and Magical Thinking, 1880–1920* (Cambridge: Cambridge University Press).
Tonning, Erik. 2014. *Modernism and Christianity* (New York: Palgrave Macmillan).
Toomey, Deirdre. 2004. 'Bowen, Elizabeth Dorothea Cole (1899–1973)'. *Oxford Dictionary of National Biography* (Oxford: Oxford University Press). https://doi.org/10.1093/ref:odnb/30839
Tracy, Robert. 1998. *The Unappeasable Host: Studies in Irish Identities* (Dublin: UCD Press).
Vetter, Lara. 2010. *Modernist Writings and Religio-Scientific Discourse: H.D., Loy and Toomer* (New York: Palgrave).
Wallace, Diana. 2004. 'Uncanny Stories: The Ghost Story as Female Gothic'. *Gothic Studies* 6 (1): 57–68.
Walsh, Keri. 2017. 'Elizabeth Bowen and the Futurist Imagination'. *Journal of Modern Literature* 41 (1): 19–39.
———. 2019. 'Elizabeth Bowen: Surrealist'. In *Elizabeth Bowen: Theory, Thought and Things* edited by Jessica Gildersleeve and Patricia Juliana Smith, 28–47. (Edinburgh: Edinburgh University Press).
Walshe, Eibhear, ed. 2009. *Elizabeth Bowen* (Dublin: Irish Academic Press).
———. 2019. '"Elsewhere": Desired Landscapes in the Writings of Elizabeth Bowen'. *The Elizabeth Bowen Review* 2 (September): 27–20. http://www.bowensociety.

com/wp-content/uploads/2017/05/The-Elizabeth-Bowen-Review-Volume-2-September-2019.pdf

Warren, Victoria. 1999. '"Experience Means Nothing Till It Repeats Itself": Elizabeth Bowen's *The Death of the Heart* and Jane Austen's *Emma*'. *Modern Language Studies* 29 (2): 131–154.

Weekes, Ann Owens. 1990. *Irish Women Writers: An Uncharted Tradition* (Lexington, KY: University of Kentucky).

Whitworth, Michael. 2001. *Einstein's Wake: Relativity, Metaphor, and Modernist Literature* (Oxford: Oxford University Press).

Wilde, Oscar. 1972. 'The Critic as Artist'. In Oscar Wilde, *Plays, Prose Writings and Poems*, 1–64. (London: J. M. Dent).

Wilkinson, Lorna. 2018. '"Thousands of avid glittering eyes": Myths, Fairy-Tales and Intelligence in the Works of Elizabeth Bowen'. *The Elizabeth Bowen Review* 1 (May): 6–19. http://www.bowensociety.com/wp-content/uploads/2017/05/The-Elizabeth-Bowen-Review-Volume-1-May-2018-1.pdf

Wills, Clair. 2007. *That Neutral Ireland: A Cultural History of Ireland During the Second World War* (London: Faber and Faber).

——. 2009. '"Half Different": The Vanishing Irish in *A World of Love*'. In *Elizabeth Bowen* edited by Eibhear Walshe, 133–49. (Dublin: Irish Academic Press).

Woolf, Virginia. 1987. *The Essays of Virginia Woolf. Volume 2, 1912–1918* edited by Andrew McNeillie (London: The Hogarth Press).

——. 1988. *The Essays of Virginia Woolf. Volume 3, 1919–1924* edited by Andrew McNeillie (London: The Hogarth Press).

——. 1994. *The Essays of Virginia Woolf. Volume 4, 1925–1928* edited by Andrew McNeillie (London: The Hogarth Press).

——. 2000. *Orlando. A Biography (*London: Vintage).

Wyatt-Brown, Anne M. 1993. 'The Liberation of Mourning in Elizabeth Bowen's *The Little Girls* and *Eva Trout*'. In *Ageing and Gender in Literature: Studies in Creativity* edited by Anne M. Wyatt-Brown and Janice Rossen, 164–86. (Charlottesville and London: University Press of Virginia).

Index

adoption, 67, 69, 90, 141–2, 146, 148–9, 151
ageing, 130–40
America, xvi, 1, 121, 142, 144, 146, 150
Anglican, 8, 141
Anglo-Irish, xiii, 2, 3, 5–7, 9–10, 14–15, 18–35, 38, 48, 52, 54, 58, 60–1, 66, 69–70, 88–90, 93, 94–103, 106, 108–10, 117, 119, 121–31, 140–2, 150
animism, 7, 22, 130, 152
antisemitism, 57, 61–2
architecture, 21, 45, 93, 153
art school, xiv, xix, 32, 46, 152
atheism, 8, 55
Austen, Jane,
    Emma, 152
    Mansfield Park, 75, 106
    Pride and Prejudice, 24, 29

Backus, Margot Gayle, 2, 23, 141
Beckett, Samuel, 1, 2, 22, 28, 30, 98, 123
Bell, The, 3, 14, 69, 80

Bennett, Andrew, 7, 37, 43, 45, 67
Bible, the, 7, 51, 127, 129–30, 148–9, 152
Big House, the, 1, 20–34, 48, 63, 66, 70, 88–90, 100–2, 105, 108–10, 116–18, 122–8
Bildungsroman, 13–34, 109
Bluemel, Kristin, 6
Bowen, Elizabeth,
    NOVELS:
    Death of the Heart, The, xv, 69–78, 89, 92, 99, 104, 114–5, 131, 139, 142, 152
    Eva Trout, or Changing Scenes, xvii, 87, 140–50, 152
    Friends and Relations, xiv, 35–44, 56, 73
    Heat of the Day, The, xvi, 6, 78, 97, 99–119, 130
    Hotel, The, xiv, 4, 13–20, 36–7, 56, 107
    House in Paris, The, xv, 57–69, 77, 87, 108, 110, 116, 148
    Last September, The, xiv, 2, 14, 16–17, 19–34, 36–7, 43,

46, 56, 60, 73, 106, 121, 150
Little Girls, The, xvii, 131–40, 142
To the North, xiv, 44–57, 152
World of Love, A, xvi, 121–131, 152

SHORT STORIES:
short stories, xiv, 79–98, 152
'Anna', 69
Ann Lee's and Other Stories, xiv, 80–1
'Attractive Modern Homes', 84–5
'The Back Drawing-Room', 88–90
'Careless Talk', 93–4
'The Cat Jumps', xv, 85–6
'A Day in the Dark', 58
Day in the Dark and Other Stories, A, xvii, 80
'Dead Mabelle', 82–3
Demon Lover and Other Stories, The, xvi, 90, 93, 104
'The Demon Lover', 92, 122
'The Disinherited', 85–6, 92
'The Dolt's Tale', 94
'The Easter Egg Party', 87
Encounters, xiv, 80–1
'Foothold', 84, 89
'The Happy Autumn Fields', 95–6
'Her Table Spread', 89–90, 142

'I Hear You Say So', 118
'The Inherited Clock', 93
'In the Square', 91
'Ivy Gripped the Steps', 92–3
Joining Charles and Other Stories, xiv, 81
'The Last Bus', 8
'The Last Night in the Old Home', 142
'The Little Girl's Room', 87–8, 135
Look At All Those Roses, xv, 90
'Look At All Those Roses', 86–7
'A Love Story', 95
'Maria', 87
'Mysterious Kôr', 91–2, 105
'Oh Madam', 94
'Recent Photograph', 81–2
'Songs My Father Sang Me', 92
'Summer Night' 14, 96–7, 142–3
'Sunday Afternoon', 94
'The Tommy Crans', 90, 148
'Unwelcome Idea', 95

DRAMA
Castle Anna, xvi
'A Nativity Play', xvii

NON FICTION
Afterthought: Pieces About Writing, xvii
'The Bend Back', 37, 123–4

INDEX

'The Big House', 102, 116
Bowen's Court, xv, 23, 27, 89, 95, 99–102, 105, 108, 111, 127, 141
'By the Unapproachable Sea', 93
Collected Impressions, xvi
'The Cult of Nostalgia', 123, 125
'Eire', 97, 102
'The Forgotten Art of Living', 72
'Home for Christmas', 136
'The Idea of France', 58
'The Idea of Home', 143
'Ireland, June 1954', 128
'Ireland Today', 122–3
'A New Ireland 1950s', 128
'Notes on Writing a Novel', 140
Pictures and Conversations, 9–11, 35, 45, 52, 65, 140
Seven Winters, xv, 102
Shelbourne, The, xvi
'The Short Story in England', 80, 99
Time in Rome, A, xvii, 54, 132, 141
'What We Need in Writing', 6
'Why I Go To the Cinema', 83

Bowen, Florence (mother), xiii, 10, 19, 74–5, 93, 102, 133–4, 138–40

Bowen, Henry (father), 51, 151
  mental illness, xiii, xiv, 10, 15, 39, 55–6, 101–2, 131, 133, 139, 141–2
Bowen's Court, xiii–xviii, 34, 99–102, 121, 124, 129
  sale of, xvi–xvii, 3, 89, 101, 131–2, 136, 138, 150
Brassard, Geneviève, xxii
British Ministry of Information, xv, 6, 94, 103–4, 109
Brontë, Charlotte
  Villette, 64

Cameron, Alan, xiv, xvi, 19, 72, 121, 129–32, 136
Catholic, xvii, 21, 27, 100, 111, 116
Chessman, Harriet, 72
childlessness, 23, 68–9, 139, 146, 149, 151
  see also infertility
children, 3, 6, 9, 17–19, 23, 31, 36, 42, 44, 58–69, 86–7, 90, 116, 127–8, 134, 136, 141
Christensen, Lis, 8
Christian, 7–8, 54, 71, 149–50
cinema, 44, 79–80, 82–3, 142, 146, 148–9, 153
class, 1, 10, 13–14, 25–7, 32–3, 35–44, 61, 69–71, 74–5, 82, 85, 91, 101, 110, 116
Coates, John, 7, 38–9, 144
Cold War, the, 124, 135

Corcoran, Neil, 1, 2, 31–2, 67–8, 101, 130, 149
Coughlan, Patricia, ix, 3, 9, 30, 36, 43
Cullingford, Elizabeth, 5, 17

D'Alton, Ian, 25
Darwood, Nicola, 8
death, xiii, xiv, xvii, 10, 19, 29, 32, 48, 52, 54, 59, 62–3, 65, 81–3, 96, 107, 112, 122–30, 135, 137–8, 141
   see also murder
Derdiger, Paula, 11, 61–2, 152
D'hoker, Elke, 153
Dickens, Charles, 145, 152
disability, 87, 98, 113, 119, 142–3, 146, 151
displacement, 30, 75, 78
   see also homelessness; refugee
divorce, 38, 102
Dublin, xiii, xv, 3, 7, 27, 102–3, 142

Eddington, Arthur, 130
Edgeworth, Maria, 21, 72
Ellmann, Maud, 7, 67, 87, 93
Emergency, the, 104, 125
   see also Second World War
England, 7, 12, 13, 18, 23–4, 34–58, 63, 74, 85, 93, 102, 110, 121, 147
espionage, 104
   see also spy

fairy tale, 8, 67, 86–7, 92, 122, 127–8, 130
fascism, 45, 60, 62, 68, 110, 113
father, 16, 72–3, 80, 113, 115, 133, 136, 138–9, 141, 143, 145
femininity, 35–56, 102
feminism, 2–4, 51, 132
First World War, xiii, xiv, 1, 9, 18, 32, 37, 48, 60, 92–3, 107, 116, 121–31, 135–6
Flaubert, Gustave, 57, 80, 105, 152
Forster, E. M., 15, 82, 139, 152
Foster, Roy, 2
France, 57–8, 102, 120
   see also Paris
Freud, Sigmund, 50, 86, 92
Fussell, Paul, 45
Futurism, 8, 46–7, 153

Gan, Wendy, 47
gender, 1, 2, 5, 22, 26–7, 30, 32–3, 112, 114, 145
ghosts, 7, 32, 83–6, 90, 92, 101, 121–31, 152
Gildersleeve, Jessica, 8–9
Glendinning, Victoria, 1, 9, 131
Gothic, 2, 6, 28, 31–2, 54, 59, 62, 64, 84, 88, 101, 127, 141

Haggard, Rider
   She, 75, 91
Hand, Derek, 33
Hepburn, Allan, 6
Hirst, Diana, 46, 152–3

INDEX

home, 2, 15, 17, 19, 25, 29, 48–9, 53–8, 62, 70, 72–3, 76–7, 81, 84–5, 99, 110, 114, 116, 148
  see also homelessness,
homelessness, xvii, 19, 20, 23, 33–4, 48, 111, 131–2, 140–50
homosexuality, 5, 142–3
Hoogland, Renée, 3, 145
Hopkins, Chris, 46
House, Humphry, xiv, 5, 69, 147
Hythe, xiii, xvii, 8, 61, 75, 93, 114, 140

identity, 2, 3, 5, 9, 15–16, 20, 30, 33, 47, 81, 92, 94–8, 99, 102, 106–8, 113, 115–16, 131, 136, 140, 142–3, 146, 150
infertility, 17, 138
Inglesby, Elizabeth, 7, 152
insanity, xxviii, 54–5, 101, 108–9, 136, 138
intergenerational conflict, 9, 25, 65, 75
intermodernism, 6
interwar, 15, 19, 25, 31, 35–56, 70, 79–90, 102, 112
IRA, 23, 25, 27, 31, 33
Irish neutrality, xv, 3, 6, 94–8, 102–4, 109–110, 122
Irish War of Independence, xiv, 14, 20–34, 100
Irish Women Writers' Club, xv, 3
Italy, xiv, 13–20, 32, 46, 81
  see also Rome

James, Henry, 15, 81, 89, 94, 139–40, 152
Johnson, Kathryn, 66–8
Jordan, Heather Bryant, 5
Joyce, James, 1, 2
  Dubliners, 80
  Ulysses, 68

Kiberd, Declan, 2
Kreilkamp, Vera, 2, 9, 20

Laird, Heather, 9
language, 2, 23, 30, 53, 74, 76, 94–8, 105, 114–5, 140–50
Lassner, Phyllis, 3, 10–11, 61–2, 64, 152
Laurence, Patricia, 9
Lawrence, D. H., 80, 145, 152
Lee, Hermione, 1
Le Fanu, Sheridan, 21, 28, 127
  Uncle Silas, 24, 64, 88
Lehmann, Rosamond, xiv, xv, 7, 139
lesbian, 3, 5, 13, 15, 50, 139, 145
Linett, Maren, 129, 143, 146
London, xiv–xvii, 6, 49, 70, 88, 90–6, 102, 104–19, 122, 124, 130

Macaulay, Rose, xiv, 15
Mansfield, Katherine, 42, 80–1, 87, 94, 152
marriage, xiv, 15–19, 28–9, 32, 35–45, 52, 64, 68, 72, 117, 124, 131, 145, 147

masculinity, 24–5, 60, 112–13
Maturin, Charles, 21, 28, 88
McCormack, W. J., 2, 90
Melero, Layla Ferrández, 13
memory, 15–16, 38, 72, 99, 122, 132, 139
Minh-ha, Trinh T., 53
miscarriage, 17, 72
modernist, 1–2, 8, 18–20, 43, 44–57, 79–80, 88, 129, 139, 152
Mooney, Sinéad, ix, xix, 22, 83, 152
mother, 3, 4, 16, 28, 32, 37–41, 44, 58–69, 72–4, 81, 87, 97, 109, 112, 114, 136–9, 145, 148
  see also motherhood
motherhood, 17, 19, 64, 68, 87–8, 115–16, 141
murder, 82, 85–7
Murdoch, Iris, 129

Nietzsche, 110, 113

O'Brien, Kate
  The Land of Spices, 145
  The Last of Summer, 114
O'Connor, Frank, xv, 79–80
O'Faoláin, Sean, xv, 80, 119
orphan, 10, 25, 49, 72, 115, 139–40
O'Toole, Tina, 3, 145

Panter-Downes, Mollie, 117
Paris, 3, 38, 55, 57–69, 106

Paris Peace Conference, xvi
Parkins, Wendy, 50
Pearson, Nels, 1, 2, 34, 63–4
Plain, Gill, 5
Poe, Edgar Allen, 31, 43
postmodernism, 140, 149
Protestant, xvii, 2, 7, 21, 28, 31, 63, 88, 100–2, 128
Proust, Marcel, 15, 93, 132, 144, 152
psychoanalysis, 3, 7–8, 83, 86

queer theory, 2, 5

Radford, Jean, 50
realism, 7, 45–6, 79, 104
Rees, Goronwy, xv, 72, 118
refugee, 10, 58, 68, 77, 128, 151
Regent's Park, xv, xvi, 59, 71–2, 104
religion, 7–8, 17, 23, 39–41, 54–5, 63, 152
revolution, 14, 16, 19, 44, 58, 60, 62–3, 71, 82
Ritchie, Charles, xv–xviii, 3–8, 10, 15, 69, 72, 118, 121, 129, 131–3, 139, 147, 151
Rome, xvi, xvii, 131–2
Rose, Jacqueline, 7, 152
Royle, Nicholas, 7, 45, 67
Russia, 14, 19, 22

Said, Edward
  'late style', 140, 142

Sarton, May, xv, 5
school, 29, 32, 74, 76, 124, 132, 135, 138–9, 143, 145
    Harpenden Hall, xiii, 134;
    Downe House, xiii, 134
Second World War, xv, 1, 3, 5, 14, 57, 62, 90–119, 136
    Dunkirk, 112–13
sexuality, 2, 3, 5, 18, 30–1, 37, 65, 97, 114, 127, 145
Shakespeare, William, 152
    Hamlet, 109
    Macbeth, 139
    The Merchant of Venice, 76
    The Tempest, 94–5, 136
    Twelfth Night, 29
shell shock, xiii, 19, 32, 142
sidhe, the, 127, 135
silence, 10, 22–3, 60, 66, 109, 114, 142, 146, 150, 153
Smith, Patricia Juliana, 9, 145
Somerville and Ross, 21, 126
spiritualism, 88, 127
spy, xv, 78, 107–10, 113–14, 118–19
stammer, xiii, 10, 113, 119, 142, 144
Stendhal, 53, 57–8
Stevens, Julie Anne, 9
Stonebridge, Lyndsey, 152
suicide, 65, 82, 83, 85, 133, 138
supernatural, 84, 86, 88, 127, 139
surrealism, 153

technology 44, 46–8, 83, 146, 150
Teekell, Anna, 105

telephone, 43–4, 46, 83–4, 123, 143
television, 142, 148
Thurschwell, Pamela, 83
time, 56, 87, 93, 121–50
Titanic, the, 116
Traherne, Thomas, 129
trauma, 1, 6, 8–10, 19, 32, 39–40, 48, 70, 83, 85, 92–3, 98, 121–51
travel, 44–56, 58, 68, 104, 123, 132
treachery, 6, 9, 17, 78, 97, 104, 106, 109–119

uncanny, the, 1, 7, 28, 42, 81–4, 87, 92, 96

visual, the, 80, 142, 144, 146, 148, 152
    visual arts, 137

Wallace, Diana, 84
Walshe, Eibhear, 2, 6
Warren, Victoria, 152
Waugh, Evelyn, 46, 139
Weekes, Ann Owens, 2
Welty, Eudora, xvi, xvii
widow, 4–5, 16, 48, 64, 108, 131–2, 138
Wilde, Oscar
    'The Critic as Artist', 125
    Picture of Dorian Gray, The, 134, 137

Wilkinson, Lorna, 67
Wills, Clair, 5, 109, 122
Woolf, Virginia, xiv, xv, 4, 6, 15, 18, 46, 103, 139, 152
   Orlando, 47

Years, The, 150
Wyatt-Brown, Anne, 11, 134

Yeats, W. B., xv, 36, 69, 88, 115, 134, 137

www.ingramcontent.com/pod-product-compliance
Lightning Source LLC
Chambersburg PA
CBHW070640300426
44111CB00013B/2189